D1525179

THE SPIDER AND THE BEE

THE SPIDER
AND THE BEE

The Artistry of Spenser's
Faerie Queene

Judith Dundas

UNIVERSITY OF ILLINOIS PRESS

Urbana and Chicago

Publication of this work was supported in part
by a grant from the Campus Research Board,
University of Illinois — Urbana-Champaign.

This book is printed on acid-free paper.

Library of Congress Cataloging in Publication Data

Dundas, Judith, 1927–
    The spider and the bee.

    Includes index.
    1.   Spenser, Edmund, 1552?–1599. Faerie queene.
2.   Spenser, Edmund, 1552?–1599—Style.   3.   Figures of
speech.   4.   Rhetoric—1500–1800.   I.   Title.
PR2358.D78   1984   821'.3   83-18253
ISBN 0-252-01118-X (alk. paper)

IN MEMORIAM

MATHILDE MARY DUNDAS

RICHARD SERLE DUNDAS

Contents

Preface   ix

Introduction   "This So Curious Networke"   1

Chapter 1   Hobgoblin or Apollo? Two Kinds of Form in *The Faerie Queene*   15

Chapter 2   "So Lively and So Like": The Pursuit of Illusion   34

Chapter 3   The Rhetoric of Illusion   68

Chapter 4   Image as Ornament   93

Chapter 5   Image as Expression   123

Chapter 6   The Poet as Painter   157

Epilogue   "Eternall Peace"   189

Excursus   Spenser and the Muses   194

Illustrations   209

General Index   225

Index to *The Faerie Queene*   230

As the stuffe
Prepared for arras pictures is no picture
Till it be formed and man hath cast the beames
Of his imaginous fancy through it. . . .

George Chapman

Arachne hauing wouen in cloth of Arras a Raine-bow of sundry silkes, it was obiected vnto hir by a Ladie more captious
then cunning, that in hir worke there wanted some colours:
for that in a Raine-bow there should bee all: Unto whom she
replyed, if the colours lacke thou lookest for, thou must
imagine that they are on the other side of the cloth: For in the
Skie wee canne discerne but one side of the Raine-bowe, and
what coloures are in the other, see wee can-not, gesse wee
may.

John Lyly

Preface

Spenser's morality of art conditions everything he wrote. To discover it is to understand why he wrote as he did, for he was not creating art as self-sufficient and autonomous, to be contemplated for its own sake, but art—it would not be too much to say—as an offering to the divine. This is no narrowly moralistic or didactic purpose; it invites richness of expression and of imagery. If it took me a long time to become clear about this fact, I still knew, even as a student struggling to write a dissertation, that what I wanted somehow to identify and pay tribute to was the artistic qualities of Spenser's imagery. Not surprisingly perhaps, that great Miltonist, Merritt Y. Hughes, who was directing my work from afar, remarked in a letter to me, "It seems to me that everything I consider moral, you consider aesthetic." Instinctively, I believed then, as I believe now, that we can only know Spenser the moralist through his art.

In the two chief directions that Spenser criticism has taken during the past few years, there are clear signs that the study of meaning has dominated all other considerations. The first direction is iconographic, following in Panofsky's footsteps and attempting to unlock the mysteries of art with the "open sesame" of the traditional meanings attached to Spenser's images. This approach has been helpful in bringing us a little closer to the mind of the sixteenth century. In this way, iconography may be said to have served an educational process for critics in bringing them to the starting point at which they may begin the business of literary criticism. Unfortunately, this kind of exegesis has too often been seen as an end in itself and has failed to illuminate artistic values and all that they imply.

The second direction has been to analyze Spenser's use of language with the kind of attention usually given to Shakespeare's language; that is to say, close reading in order to find multiple meanings and patterns of significance. Although this particular critical trend passes for reading the poetry as poetry, it still focuses primarily on meaning, especially psychological meaning, rather than on style, or that aspect of meaning which derives from the special "handwriting" of the artist: his choice of forms and the way these are modified by his own artistic purpose.

Meaning as an extractable residue from poetry is itself something of a banality. Conventional allegorical and archetypal interpretation seems to have reached a dead end. Partly in response to this impasse, the so-called actual experience of reading *The Faerie Queene* has recently begun to attract critics who remain preoccupied with meaning but wish to express it either in terms of the "self-referentiality" of the text or its "fractured" state. Rejecting closed meanings, they open the way to a void of unmeaning, which denies not only Spenser's expressed purpose but the entire humanistic tradition of art. The moral implications of their approach have yet to be explored. Meanwhile, in pursuit of my own concerns, I return to a forceful reminder of a question that still has not been sufficiently addressed in Spenser criticism. It occurs at the end of A. C. Hamilton's summary of the present state

of Spenser scholarship in his edition of *The Faerie Queene:*
"What still remains unclear is the nature of the pleasure
which the poem provides and the relation of this pleasure to
its meaning."

As artist, Spenser's purpose was to achieve beauty; like
Sidney, he looked upon this as peculiarly the poet's task. Yet
what much Spenser criticism implies—encouraged no doubt
by iconographic and archetypal methods—is that his moral
message may be divorced from his concern with beauty, or
may even be opposed to this same love of beauty. Spenser
himself, in the spirit of Plato, prefers to see beauty and goodness as one:

> Him to behold, is on his workes to looke,
> Which he hath made in beauty excellent,
> And in the same, as in a brasen booke,
> To reade enregistred in every nooke
> His goodnesse, which his beautie doth declare,
> For all thats good is beautifull and faire.
> (*HHB*.128–33)

In other words, his view of art is essentially religious—that
art ought to be in the service of truth, not in the service of
falsehood. He cannot treat beauty as an end in itself but only
as a worshipful manifestation from on high. Like the craftsmanship of the Gothic cathedral, in its elegant lines and glis-
tening lights, his art makes beauty a conduit for the divine.

To see how art functions in the service of truth may in turn
provide a way of seeing why it sometimes does not. If
Spenser makes his own illusion, he also supplies a critique of
the illusion which evil genius can produce at will. He knows
whereof he speaks; he, the artist, knows what power is there
to be unleashed for good or evil. The morality of art is his
abiding concern. But how can we understand this unless we
try to see what his own conception of art is? Does the evil art

differ significantly from the good art, or are their means identical? His own practice may give an answer to some of these perplexing questions. Not without reason critics have often been baffled by his treatment of that beauty spot, the Bower of Bliss. The aesthetics of *The Faerie Queene* must differ in some profound sense from those of the Bower; otherwise, his whole message loses its meaning. In the end, he must supply us with a means of discriminating between the pure and the impure uses of art.

But for the moment, it is enough that we recognize that, for Spenser, to beautify by all the formal means at his disposal was his merest obligation to the truth. His fondness for the words *beauty* and *beautify* can be documented—they occur some 212 times in his poems—but his references to such related concepts as craftsmanship and skill are so numerous as to set aside statistics and reveal the poet of the beautiful in his own artistic aims and desires. I do not propose to examine all his methods of beautifying his work, which would have to include the use of sound patterns, and many more rhetorical devices than those I mention. My inquiry is limited to those aspects of his artistic purpose that particularly concern the form of his imagery.

Like all Renaissance artists, he is intent on creating an illusion of reality: "So lively and so like" might almost be the motto for his work as a whole. Although it is tempting to borrow from studies in perception and treat the psychology of representation in literature as though it were the same as the psychology of representation in art, it has to be recognized that pictures evoked in the imagination are not governed by the same laws as illusion in painting. If we were to wait for psychologists to tell us precisely how literature works on our visual imaginations, we might have to wait for a very long time. This kind of information is simply not available, as it has, for example, been available to E. H. Gombrich for the study of illusion in painting. Fortunately, literary criticism need not wait for psychology to provide information about the effect of language on perception. The whole rhetorical tradition is concerned with nothing else.

Here I must acknowledge my debt to Rosemond Tuve's *Elizabethan and Metaphysical Imagery;* yet my purpose is rather different from hers. Essentially, her book is a demonstration of the need to understand Renaissance imagery according to the rhetorical criteria of the time, instead of according to modern critical assumptions. Her argument, however, requires that she subordinate the decorative and sensuous qualities of images to their logical function within a poem. I am more concerned with what may be called their affective function. Defending Renaissance descriptive images on grounds of their logical value may simply skirt the problem of aesthetic response.

If we are to read Spenser as a poet, we must, I believe, attend to the kind of beauty he evokes. I have centered my attention, then, on the artistic assumptions which underlie his work and on the way these affect his imagery in particular. My introduction interprets my emblematic title and suggests its relevance to Spenser's use of expressive and restrictive form. The operation of these opposed but complementary principles in *The Faerie Queene* as a whole is illustrated in the first chapter. In the following chapter, Spenser's view of illusionistic art and his own pursuit of it are examined. The next three chapters deal specifically with rhetorical aspects of his imagery: his use of descriptive schemes, his ornamental style, and his expressive purpose. Finally, in my last chapter, I return to the essential mystery of artistic illusion, which not even rhetoric can fully explain and which must therefore be attributed to the Muses.

Acknowledgments

I am grateful to the editors of *Studies in English Literature* and *Modern Philology* for permission to include material in Chapters 1 and 3 which was originally published in article form in these journals.* I also wish to thank the Research Board of the University of Illinois at Urbana-Champaign for their assistance. John Kevin Newman kindly provided translations for the inscriptions on the engravings reproduced in Figures 3 and 6.

Reproductions by kind permission of the following: the University of Illinois Library (Fig. 1), the British Library (Figs. 2 and 5), the Rijksmuseum (Fig. 3), Böhm, Venice (Fig. 4), The Metropolitan Museum of Art, Harris Brisbane Dick Fund, 1953 [53.601.337(7)] (Fig. 6).

My chief debt in the working out of my ideas is to two people, neither of them Spenserians, who were probably not even conscious that they were contributing to this work. They are Sir Ernst Gombrich and Philipp Fehl. To meet them

*Reprinted from *SEL*, 8 (1968), 59–75, and from *MP*, 71 (1974), 257–65: excerpts. By permission of the University of Chicago Press. ©1974 by The University of Chicago.

was to find fellow workers in another part of the vineyard. At a later stage, three Spenserians came to my aid: A. C. Hamilton, Hugh Maclean, and A. Kent Hieatt. If my musings have seen the light of day, it is at least partly owing to their mediating efforts.

"This So Curious Networke"

The spider's web and the honeycomb of the bee imply in various ways Spenser's view of the artist's task, including his own. Believing as I do on the basis of all his work that he was not concerned either with discovering himself or with self-contemplation but with making his poem a fit representation of moral truth, I have chosen these insect images, which he himself uses, to suggest that we look at *The Faerie Queene* as his artistic problem rather than his psychological one.

Spenser's references to the spider's web and to the honeycomb show the craftsman at work on an ordered design with a particular purpose. If the poet himself becomes part of the design, the aspect of himself he chooses to show must be compatible with that design. Colin Clout as representative pastoral poet fits neatly into the pastoral episode of Book VI; his presence does not necessarily prove that Spenser has made his own voice clearer, or that he has turned from the external world more exclusively to his inner life. The entire poem refers to the relationship between the inner life and the outer world of action. Withdrawal, whether into contemplation or into pastoral content, can be no true goal for the hero, whose symbol of the sword in hand marks him off from the world of religious or aesthetic contemplation. But the poet, too, has his call to confront the world; lacking a sword, he holds another weapon in the web he weaves. With that, he enthralls the reader, holding in his hand all the threads of his story and acting as sole arbiter of the world he creates.

It is true that the poet, like anyone else, may grow weary or despondent about the actual world, but more important artistically, he may grow weary of his task because he cannot find his way out of the maze of confusion, cannot find an adequate myth—everything summed up in saying that his invention fails him. It was this fear, I believe, that may have overshadowed the last part of *The Faerie Queene,* rather than events in Spenser's world of experience. At least for the purpose of criticism, perhaps we should pay more attention to the adequacy of his myths and his design, rather than speculating about his voyage of self-discovery and where that may have brought him.

Traditionally, the bee's craftsmanship serves as a model of the order to which poets, as well as rulers, might aspire. In John Lyly's words: "Euery one hath his office, some trimming the honny, some working the wax, one framing hiues, an other the combes, and that so artificially, that *Dedalus* could not with greater arte or excellencie, better dispose the orders, measures, proportions, distinctions, ioynts, & circles."[1] For Colin Clout, the disappointed and disillusioned poet, the bee is a reminder of his earlier, more productive days:

> Where I was wont to seeke the honey bee,
> Working her formall rowmes in wexen frame.
> (*SC.*Dec.67–68)[2]

Spenser too makes "formall rowmes" both in the stanzas and in the books of *The Faerie Queene;* for him, the schema was a necessity, no matter how mechanical. His *Calender,* for ex-

ample, uses the framework of the months to give a structure
to a disparate collection of lyrics and satires. His *Amoretti*
puts his own love story into the rooms of his sonnet form, so
that sentiment is contained and multiplied through eighty-
eight self-contained, parallel, yet sequential units. When he
praises architecture, it is not only for richness but also, typi-
cally, for orderly arrangement:

> beholding all the way
> The goodly workes, and stones of rich assay,
> Cast into sundry shapes by wondrous skill,
> That like on earth no where I recken may.
> *(FQ.4.10.15)*

The Temple of Venus, as Sir Scudamore describes it, has the
quality of Spenser's own workmanship, of laying words side
by side to form "sundry shapes by wondrous skill."

The workmanship of the bee thus represents one part at
least of Spenser's artistic concern: joining small, self-contained units to make bigger ones. More important, it suggests
the whole rhetorical tradition of selecting and arranging,
of using predetermined forms, including topoi and conventional structures, in order to hold the honey of the poet's
eloquence.

This honey itself is culled from the works of other poets.
The bee is also a familiar model for poets in their work of
imitating their great predecessors, as Seneca indicates in a
classic statement applicable to all writers:

> We should follow, men say, the example of the bees,
> who flit about and cull the flowers that are suitable for
> producing honey, and then arrange and assort in their
> cells all that they have brought in; these bees, as our
> Vergil says, 'pack close the flowing honey, / And swell
> their cells with nectar sweet.'

> . . . We also, I say, ought to copy these bees, and sift whatever we have gathered from a varied course of reading, for such things are better preserved if they are kept separate; then, by applying the supervising care with which our nature has endowed us,—in other words, our natural gifts,—we should so blend those several flavours into one delicious compound that, even though it betrays its origin, yet it nevertheless is clearly a different thing from that whence it came.[3]

At this point, Seneca stresses the need to "digest" what we borrow, "otherwise it will merely pass into the memory and not enter into our very being." We should reveal only what we have made of our borrowings, not the borrowings themselves. In still another metaphor, he compares the resemblance of the new creation to a child's resemblance to its father.

It is clear that the possibilities suggested by the bee as a model for poets are limited: its patient industry and the symmetrical order of its craft will hardly suffice for a great work of art. If they would, *The Teares of the Nine Muses* or *The Ruines of Time* would be more successful poems than they are. For Spenser, a bigger symbol is needed to encompass his purpose in *The Faerie Queene* and the intricacy of his art. Both historically and personally, a more important symbol for the poet's craft is the spider and his web, akin as it is to the tapestry of the world as woven by the gods and the "picture-world of tapestry" woven by mortals.[4] For the ancients, including Homer, the web or tapestry represented the illusion-making craft, the spell that the bard cast over his audience. In *The Odyssey,* for example, we find a reference to the gods as weavers of man's fate and to the poet as a weaver of song (VIII). In one of Spenser's dedicatory sonnets to *The Faerie Queene,* he makes a conventional apology for his art by referring to the "Rude rymes, the which a rustick Muse did weave / In savadge soyle, far from Parnasso mount, / And roughly wrought in an unlearned loome." A similar apology, taken from his Latin original, *The Culex,* opens *Virgils Gnat:*

> We now have playde (Augustus) wantonly,
> Tuning our song unto a tender Muse,
> And like a cobweb weaving slenderly,
> Have onely playde. . . .
>
> (ll. 1–4)

Despite the numerous poetic allusions to the thinness of the spider's web as like the fragility of the poet's art, Spenser delights in the paradox of strength in weakness. In his *Visions of the Worlds Vanitie,* he has a whole series of exempla to illustrate how often the strong are overcome by the weak, including a tale of a dragon which was subdued by the venom of a spider (VI). It is a reminder that we cannot judge by appearances, that we live in a world of dangerous illusion, and that the poet's work is to cleanse us of false illusion by making an illusion which contains the truth.

A net is needed to counter a net; the poet's seemingly weak web, if woven skillfully enough, can present a counter-illusion to the illusion of this world. For Spenser the word "skill," a key one in *The Teares of the Muses,* means more than craftsmanship: the "sacred skill" of the poet puts him on the side of God. Yet even the evil use of web-making skill calls for admiration. Vida, in recommending insects and small creatures as suitable subjects for the budding poet, had particularly mentioned the spider: "Or with what art her toils the spider sets, / And spins her filmy entrails into nets."[5] Spenser was perhaps following Vida's advice—who followed Virgil— in a larger way, by writing the fate of the butterfly before *The Faerie Queene;* and in a smaller way, by showing in *Muiopotmos* how exquisite the workmanship of the spider is:

And weaving straight a net with manie a folde
About the cave in which he lurking dwelt,
With fine small cords about it stretched wide,
So finely sponne that scarce they could be spide.

Not anie damzell, which her vaunteth most
In skilfull knitting of soft silken twyne;
Nor anie weaver, which his worke doth boast
In dieper, in damaske, or in lyne;
Nor anie skil'd in workmanship embost;
Nor anie skil'd in loupes of fingring fine,
Might in their divers cunning ever dare,
With this so curious networke to compare.

                                        (ll. 357–68)

Malice and deceit, as Spenser well knew, are quite compatible with fine workmanship. Besides the spider, Detraction delights to weave her false tales to ensnare the innocent
(*FQ*.5.12.36). More notably, in the Bower of Bliss, Acrasia's
dress acts as a trap for the pleasure-loving:

More subtile web Arachne cannot spin,
Nor the fine nets, which oft we woven see
Of scorched deaw, do not in th' ayre more lightly flee.

                                        (2.12.77)

Only the palmer's net, modeled on that of Vulcan in which he
caught Venus and Mars, can match Acrasia's for subtlety:

suddein forth they on them rusht and threw
A subtile net, which only for that same
The skilfull palmer formally did frame.

                                        (2.12.81)

Ironically, these "captive bandes" are like the bands of
love. In a number of the *Amoretti,* love sets traps, so that it
seems perfectly natural for Spenser to allude to the web that
Penelope wove to deceive her suitors as his beloved's own

form of deceit; he himself has also been engaged in making
his trap for her:

> For with one looke she spils that long I sponne,
> And with one word my whole years work doth rend.
> Such labour like the spyders web I fynd,
> Whose fruitless worke is broken with least wynd.
>
> (*Am.*23)

His self-identification with the spider in his capacity as lover
reaches its humorous climax in sonnet 71, where an actual
tapestry unites two opposite and yet complementary insects:[6]

> I joy to see how, in your drawen work,
> Your selfe unto the bee ye doe compare,
> And me unto the spyder, that doth lurke
> In close awayt to catch her unaware.
> Right so your selfe were caught in cunning snare
> Of a deare foe, and thralled to his love:
> In whose streight bands ye now captived are
> So firmely, that ye never may remove.
> But as your worke is woven all above
> With woodbynd flowers and fragrant eglantine,
> So sweet your prison you in time shall prove,
> With many deare delights bedecked fyne:
> And all thensforth eternall peace shall see
> Betweene the spyder and the gentle bee.

When the patient industry of the gentle bee is combined with
the magical spinning of the less gentle spider, we have a total
image not only for Spenser's love but also for his art.

What the poet makes is "a subtile net" to catch his reader.
Just as the net framed by the palmer is of the spirit, so the net
framed by the poet is also the weapon of heaven. Here it
must be noted that the "guilefull trap" always serves God's
purposes, whether set by the good palmer or the evil spider.
The net of Acrasia's gown is no less a trap for sinners than

Aragnoll's spiderweb which catches the erring butterfly of *Muiopotmos.* Or we may think of Mammon's cave, where the Arachne image is introduced to indicate that this place is a trap for sinners, as well as to show the decay and desolation born of riches. Man readily falls into a labyrinth from which he can find no escape, but by weaving a song the poet may construct a labyrinth for himself and his audience, with the vital clue remaining in his hand, even though he may not fully understand the riddle he himself has made.

Weaving as a metaphor implies separate strands; he who weaves creates an order based on the opposites of warp and woof. There is thus a complexity in the spider's web which does not exist in the bee's honeycomb. Insofar as the poet is like the bee, he constructs formal rooms which he fills with honey; insofar as he is like the spider, he weaves a web to catch the reader.[7] The latter is the more creative and more dangerous image, and perhaps Spenser could not use it directly for himself except in the context of humorous love sonnets. He could, and did, however, use the image of the weaver, which is the more purified and less dangerous form of the spider image.

In this, he follows both classical tradition and such Renaissance poets as Ariosto, who used the metaphor to refer to the illusion they were creating. Ariosto, for example, after one of his customary addresses to his audience, takes up his story again by saying: "But now to return to the story which I am weaving from various strands" (*Orlando Furioso.*22.3). It is a metaphor specially appropriate to the romance technique of interlace, by which various stories are kept in motion at the same time. The poet becomes a magician, a conjurer, as we watch him in the act of weaving his tapestry and bringing into existence something out of nothing by the sheer power of his words.

In the tradition of medieval romance, the storyteller is more conspicuous as the spinner of his tale than either epic poet or modern novelist, no doubt because his scene is less situated in history or in the world of everyday life, and the underlying pattern, or mystery of purpose, is hidden from all but him. We do not know what adventures Sir Guyon must have before he can achieve his quest of finding and destroying the Bower of Bliss, or where or how Britomart will meet her Artegall. It is a sign of the storyteller's skill that in a world apparently governed by chance, in which characters crisscross the waste wilderness encountering other characters, he can hold all the threads of the different stories in his hand at once and give the effect of simultaneity for events that must of necessity be recorded sequentially. The whole cloth is there, even if we never see it whole, and any part will carry conviction as belonging to that whole.

If then the honeycomb makes us think of the structure of parts, the web makes us think of the poet's entire creation, with its power over our imaginations. Yet these are not quite distinguishable as means and end, but rather as two different ways of viewing the poem, the one as design, the other as illusion. It is only when Spenser too dutifully fills his conventional moulds, as in some of his battle scenes, that we may feel that the bee has the upper hand; in general, bee and spider live together as harmoniously as he sees them doing in Elizabeth Boyle's tapestry.

At their best, fantasy and formulation can produce the dreams of those that are awake, as the poet responds both to the romance situations and to the allegorical figures who fit so easily into them. We cannot begin to consider the rightness of the images except as they make their desired effect of creating the illusion that we are actually witnessing something. But to interpret this imaginary visual experience as if it were governed by anything resembling the laws of visual perception is to proceed on the basis of an analogy that imposes alien rules upon the poet's form of creation. It is better to look to literary tradition rather than to the psychology of perception; at least we come closer to the kind of assumptions Spenser worked from.

He does not think about the way we perceive things but about the way a storyteller proceeds, carried along by the events of his tale; this gives the groundwork of his imagery. Then if he wishes to dwell upon something particularly beautiful, or ugly, or significant, he may pause to enumerate features, or to amplify by similes. Always, he thinks of arranging his words to fit his stanza, to make a decorative pattern, not to duplicate visual experience but to stir the imagination, the inner sight, by allusion, suggestion, but at the same time by definition which seems to assert the existence of something that only his words can evoke.

But the reality of his fairyland is asserted not as dream vision but as simple fact. Since this is in the oldest and best tradition of storytelling, we may gain some help—certainly more than from modern studies of perception—from critics in the classical tradition, such as Junius; he refers to poets who "impelled by the sudden heate of a thoroughly stirred Phantasie, or rather transposed by a prophetic traunce doe clearly behold the round rings of prettily dancing Nymphs."[8] We think of Spenser's "hundred naked maidens lilly white, / All raunged in a ring, and dauncing in delight." He creates the apparition, not by details but by phrases containing key allusions to such crucial features as whiteness and dancing in a circle. Although totally conventional, the description has the power of revelation through the wonder expressed by the precise choice of words, their order, and their rhythm.

There is no call to be naturalistic in Spenser's world, but, equally, there is no call to make purely artificial symbols. He

maintains the fiction of oral narration, while shaping everything not only for significance but also for beauty. His engagement is manifest in a thousand small ways, such as the
realism of the Polyphemus-figure of Lust who holds the captive Amoret as a buckler, "Whilest thus"—fortuitously Belphoebe appears as Chastity to defeat Lust of his prey. Such
images would not have their fantasy power if it were not for
Spenser's ability to make his schemata serve his imagination.

That he needed schemata—the honeycomb—is beyond
question, writing as he did at a time when the rational purposes of art and the acceptance of traditional modes of expression made it inevitable. And Renaissance psychology,
too, presents an analogy to artistic procedure by holding that
what the imagination took from the senses and purified, the
intellect could contemplate as in a mirror, selecting whatever
it needed for the work of art.[9] Within the framework devised
by reason, fantasy could have free play; as an uncontrolled or
undirected faculty, on the other hand, it is like the swarming
of bees or the buzzing of flies.[10] Ordinarily, the fantasy image
could not initiate art, because Minerva, not Fortune, rules in
this sphere.[11]

Within his finite forms, Spenser sees himself as compres-
sing the infinite. Speaking of his task of naming all the famous rivers who attended the wedding of the Medway and
Thames, he asks:

> How can they all in this so narrow verse
> Contayned be, and in small compasse hild?
> (4.11.17)

Elsewhere, he laments what escapes his "afflicted style" and
how insufficient his pen is to express the purity of his
queen—his fear "through want of words, her excellence to
marre." His awareness of the problem of expression goes beyond conventional humility because, as his allegory alone

would have reminded him, he was committed to limited forms for the expression of infinite truth.

Nevertheless, it is from these limited forms that Spenser creates the poetic illusion which is his great achievement. Just as invention did not mean creating out of nothing but finding a new way of conceiving an old subject, so the old topoi and rhetorical forms can be made to live with a new beauty and significance when they take their place in what Sidney calls "a good invention," or a fiction that is true. But it becomes true only in the handling of it; expression thus resolves itself into the problem of making the right choices from all the means available. To show what is eternally true in romance situations, Spenser had to relive them; but as a very conscious artist, he had also to select, shape, and define his traditional images so as to bring out their truth more clearly and beautifully. The result in *The Faerie Queene* is an illusionistic narrative which is also patterned symbolically and decoratively. And if this seems a contradiction in terms, it simply points to the same paradox suggested by the images of bee and spider: the conservative, imitative impulse of the poet, on the one hand, and the imaginative power which casts a spell over the reader, on the other hand. The following chapters will pose the question of how Spenser attempted to reconcile the spider and the bee in his own tapestry and will suggest some answers.

NOTES

1. John Lyly, *Euphues and his England,* in *The Complete Works,* ed. R. Warwick Bond (Oxford, 1902), 2:45. See also Pliny, *Natural History,* XI.x.22–24.

2. All quotations from Spenser are taken from *The Complete Poetical Works of Spenser,* ed. R. E. N. Dodge (Boston, 1936).

3. Seneca, *Epistulae Morales,* trans. Richard M. Gummere, Loeb Classical Library (New York, 1920), 2:277 and 279. For other references to the poet as bee in his task of literary imitation, see R. J. Clements, *Critical Theory and Practice of the Pléiade* (Cambridge, Mass., 1942), pp. 168–75, and his *Picta Poesis* (Rome, 1960), pp. 184–85. On bees as "Birds of the Muses," see Hilda M. Ransome, *The Sacred Bee in Ancient Times and Folklore* (London, 1937), pp. 103–6.

4. Rhys Carpenter's expression in *The Esthetic Basis of Greek Art* (Bloomington, Ind., 1959), p. 46.

5. Vida, *Art of Poetry,* trans. Christopher Pitt, in Albert S. Cook, *The Art of Poetry* (Boston, 1892), 1:467–68, p. 69.

6. Instead of the word "about" at the end of the ninth line, I have substituted the emendation "above," which is accepted by the Spenser Variorum and which preserves the rhyme.

If not exactly friendly insects in Lyly's proverb lore, the spider and the bee at least do not attack one another: "though the Spyder poyson the Flie, she cannot infect the Bee" (*Euphues: The Anatomy of Wyt,* in *Complete Works,* 1:206). It has been suggested that the spider and the bee of this sonnet allude playfully to the first letters of Spenser's surname and of "Boyle," the surname of his fiancée. But the subject of Elizabeth Boyle's tapestry also recalls the Elizabethan fondness for insects as decorative and symbolic motifs. Joan Evans in her *Nature in Design* (Oxford, 1933) notes that Queen Elizabeth had a dress embroidered with spiders, flies, and other insects (p. 98). These little creatures, even some of the most despised, such as worms, had the same role that they played in medieval manuscripts and sculpture.

7. The distinction between spider (or silkworm) and bee as representing artists who followed tradition and those who invented or discovered their own artistic principles is discussed in Baxter Hathaway, *The Age of Criticism* (Ithaca, 1962), pp. 449–51. However, my distinction differs in treating the spider in the more primitive sense of spinner and therefore maker of illusions. Cf. Sidney's dedication of his *Arcadia* to his sister, in which he refers to "this idle work of mine,

which, I fear, like the spider's web, will be thought fitter to be swept away than worn to any other purpose."

8. See Franciscus Junius, *The Painting of the Ancients* (London, 1638), I.4.6.

9. See, for example, Marsilio Ficino, *Commentary on Plato's Symposium,* trans. Sears Jayne (Columbia, Mo., 1944), p. 189.

10. *FQ*.2.9.51.

11. See, for example, Plutarch's essay "Of Fortune," in his *Moralia,* trans. Philemon Holland, Everyman's Library ed. (London, [1911]), p. 319.

CHAPTER I

Hobgoblin or Apollo?
Two Kinds of Form in
The Faerie Queene

I

S penser's story is the dynamic or expressive form of his poem. I have called it a web to catch the reader. When, in his prefatory letter to *The Faerie Queene,* he speaks of "the use of these dayes," when all things are "accounted by their showes, and nothing esteemed of, that is not delightfull and pleasing to commune sence," he is admitting the chief factor in his choice of romance form: its popular appeal derived from the variety of its action. His deprecating words conceal his recognition of the value, to him as poet and to us as readers, of a story which will carry us along. They also imply that his imagery must first of all be subordinated to the needs of his story; it can enjoy no other kind of freedom.

But considerable as this freedom is, it is subject to a restriction which the ordinary writer of fiction does not have to observe. I refer of course to Spenser's allegory. He gives this primacy in explaining the purpose of his poem: "to fashion a gentle man or noble person in vertuous and gentle discipline." Through his allegory he can relate his poem to human life in the way he believes it should be related, and in this he shows his adherence to the entire humanist tradition. At the same time, his allegorical scheme serves artistic ends, as well as moral ends. Through it, he is able to give a rational order to the irrational events of his fairyland. The effect on his narrative imagery is to turn it toward emblem and symbol, always implicitly and frequently explicitly, with the help of names of characters and places, such as Duessa and the House of Pride, or with the help of mottoes, such as "God helpe the man so wrapt in Errours endlesse traine," where the moralizing statement or "sentence" explains the image, as the image explains the "sentence." By imposing the schematic form of his allegory on his narrative, Spenser in effect turned his images into self-contained units, fitted together like the cells of a honeycomb. An order of this kind, more spatial in its design than the time order of narrative, sets limits not only to separate images but also to the larger divisions of the poem, the separate books. In so joining the restrictive order of allegory with the expressive order of narrative, Spenser is perfectly in accord with Elizabethan theories of poetry.

For the Renaissance poet, as for the Renaissance painter, invention was the first and most crucial step in the making of a work of art. It represents the essence of his conception—what Sidney calls the poet's "fore-conceit"—before he has given it actual form, and it joins two faculties of the mind which might otherwise be opposed: reason and imagination.[1] In part, the methods of oratorical *inventio,* consisting in running over in one's mind the most appropriate arguments for a case, underline the importance of "imitation" in artistic invention; the precedents set by previous writers, as well as the store of commonplaces which every artist possessed, served as stimuli to composition. But because invention was not merely imitation, it required imagination in order to attain "depth of device," or new and subtle conjunctions of ideas. In Puttenham's defense of imagination or fantasy, he refers to people who are "illuminated with the brightest irradiations of knowledge and the veritie and proportions of things" as *euphansiote,* "and of this sorte of phantasie are all good Poets, notable Captaines strategematique, all cunning artificers and enginers, all Legislators Politiens & Counsellors of estate, in whose exercise the inuentiue part is most employed and is to the sound and true iudgement of man most needful."[2] He thus makes "phantasie and imagination" a mirror of truth, which the more rational part of the mind must seek out the best means of making visible to the reader or audience. It is this kind of inventive ability that E. K. praises when he refers to Spenser's "wittiness in devising."[3]

　Inevitably, the means of "bodying forth" an idea would, in the Renaissance, suggest itself in terms of genre.[4] Indeed, so much was invention dependent upon the various genres that poetic composition seems often to have begun with the desire to write a sonnet, a mythological poem, an epic, rather than with an idea. Of course, it is difficult, or impossible, to separate the two. Did Spenser begin with the desire to write an epic or with the purpose of praising virtue and condemning vice?[5] Given his historical period, the one is as likely as the other. His great invention, however, is to make the stories of chivalric romance live again with the enriched significance they gain from allegory. In practice, he takes what is implicit in romance and makes it both more explicit and more ordered, with the result that he reinvents his genre, just as Dante reinvented his. No doubt this is true of every great work of art, but it remains a matter of interest to try to see how this should be, especially as our definition of Spenser's genre is intimately related not only to the way we read his poem but even to the way we interpret its incompleteness.

Here, too, in the shaping of his genre, we may begin to look for the conditions under which his imagery is formed and the ends it is designed to meet.

It is clear not only from the prefatory letter but from the entire corpus of Spenser's work that the ideal exercised such a hold over his imagination that he could only write an epic in praise of truth, beauty, goodness. But that in itself is a novelty, for most epics, from Homer to Milton, assume some kind of historical past as the basis for the narrative. To write an epic in praise of the ideal must necessarily remove the story from the context of history, since history can at best provide only notable examples of virtue, not the virtues in their absolute form.

Outside of history, there is room in an epic only for either the narrative of fantasy or of dream vision, the latter carrying its own authority as serious narrative. But the apocalyptic nature of dream vision does not allow for the ideal to be seen here below, on earth, unless it be as divinity. Only fantasy provides the freedom to make the virtues walk the earth. And it was fortunate for Spenser that the romance of chivalry was still viable as a shared fantasy concerned with ideal themes and still having a semblance of historical milieu—the Middle Ages—which provided the details for a verisimilar narrative, complete with customs and attire, with dwelling places, and with the elements of a conventional geography. No private fantasy can probably present such an illusion of an objective reality.

For this reality, the sureness of description, even when details are few and vague, is eloquent testimony. Insofar as Spenser's images reflect in some measure this shared fantasy, he has a sanction for them far more compelling than any allegorical label can give them. Orgoglio, for example, is first and foremost a terrifying giant who has come upon Red

Cross when the knight is at his most vulnerable, "disarmd, disgraste, and inwardly dismayde":

> But ere he could his armour on him dight,
> Or gett his shield, his monstrous enimy
> With sturdie steps came stalking in his sight,
> An hideous geaunt, horrible and hye,
> That with his tallnesse seemd to threat the skye;
> The ground eke groned under him for dreed:
> His living like saw never living eye,
> Ne durst behold: his stature did exceed
> The hight of three the tallest sonnes of mortall seed.
>
> (1.7.8)

After two lines of introduction, the rest of the stanza is taken up with attempting to convey the terror inspired by the giant's extreme height, and it is the knight's terror which dictates the storyteller's choice of words, including the adjectives "monstrous," "hideous," "horrible," which underline the connotations of "stalking." Although the language has the familiar formulaic ring, as well as the tendency to generalize, it paints a vivid picture because the poet has succeeded in reviving the words in which the original fantasy image was encapsulated. In this revival of the fantasy image lies the visual impact of Spenser's poem; not for nothing did Renaissance critics like the etymological link between fantasy and sight.[6] Here the web is woven to entrap the reader, and here the poem must stand or fall as a work of art, however much the shaping hand of the artist is called into play.

If we consider the description of Phantastes in the Castle of Alma, it seems only a disorderly faculty:

> His chamber was dispainted all with in
> With sondry colours, in the which were writ
> Infinite shapes of thinges dispersed thin;

Some such as in the world were never yit,
Ne can devized be of mortall wit;
Some daily seene, and knowen by their names,
Such as idle fantasies doe flit:
Infernall hags, centaurs, feendes, hippodames,
Apes, lyons, aegles, owles, fooles, lovers, children, dames.

And all the chamber filled was with flyes,
Which buzzed all about, and made such sound,
That they encombred all mens eares and eyes,
Like many swarmes of bees assembled round,
After their hives with honny do abound:
All those were idle thoughtes and fantasies,
Devices, dreames, opinions unsound,
Shewes, visions, sooth-sayes, and prophesies;
And all that fained is, as leasings, tales, and lies.

(2.9.50–51)

Yet fantasy need not be merely the buzzing of flies or the swarming of bees; it may be expressed in a more orderly way through story. So natural to the human mind is this method of ordering that we all tell ourselves stories in our dreams, as well as in our daytime musings. For Spenser, much depends upon finding the right story for his particular purpose at a given moment, but he had already made his great commitment when he chose chivalric romance as his symbolic medium. As John Hughes in his eighteenth-century edition of *The Faerie Queene* remarks, "the chief Reason" that Spenser chose romance "was probably, that he chose to frame his Fable after a Model which might give the greatest Scope to that Range of Fancy which was so remarkably his Talent."[7] Hughes uses the word "frame," which implies structure or a purposeful order, but at the same time he notes the expressive qualities of the romance genre, its receptivity to images of all kinds.

Since the appearance of freedom is essential to a work which depends so heavily upon Hobgoblin, Spenser wisely followed Ariosto's lead in using the interlace pattern of narrative.[8] It conveys a sense of the unexpected, even random occurrence of events and is hospitable to all the images of fairy-tale life. This interweaving of separate strands also suggests an endlessness, a linear progression for which there is no inevitable conclusion. Paradoxically, the writer's freedom provides the reader's compulsion, as we are carried along by something seemingly uncontrollable, an invisible energy which finds its outlet in a stream of images that do not belong to our waking life but are nonetheless familiar. Of course the writer controls the weaving of his stories; what is important is that a sense of order should not obtrude too much. Where too much control is evident and the stories lack an expansive beauty, as in the exempla at the beginning of Book V, the poet partly loses his hold over the reader's imagination, which requires the unlimited and even the chaotic to feel perfectly at home.

What is needed, as I have said, is the appearance of freedom, not the fact. In Book I, the appearance is beautifully preserved, with the separation and reuniting of Una and Red Cross, and the interlaced appearances and disappearances of Archimago and Duessa conforming, as it seems, to the inner life of the imagination. The effect of simultaneity is sustained through flashbacks and recapitulations, as well as by transitional expressions of the "meanwhile" sort. One feels that Spenser has his threads well under control and never drops a stitch. The patterning of good and evil heightens, rather than destroys, the vitality of the images. In part, at least, the success of Book I is due to Spenser's luck in finding the right myth for his purposes; he was not always so lucky in the other books and had to improvise with a combination of romantic

narrative and exempla. But in every book he tries to provide
for both narrative continuity and freedom by means of the
interwoven method.

The journey, which provides the essential element of continuity in the narrative, lends itself naturally to a succession
of episodes, but the idea that there is a hidden plan in human
affairs, that Divine Providence oversees everything, finds expression in the quest motif. Whatever disjunction there may
be between the events of a book and the quest of the hero,
the wanderings of the titular knight are given a purposeful-
ness which is somehow in keeping with the divine plan. At
the same time, the quest does not interfere with the poet's
narrative freedom, as a more insistent plot might; rather, it
gives him unlimited opportunity for variety of incident and
unexpected encounters. Since the hero is never sure where
his quest is taking him, every moment becomes equally full
of potential for a moral triumph or defeat, as the case may be.
Above all, the quest, along with the interlace design, is perfectly attuned to the aimlessness of fantasy, the dreamlike
meanderings which Minturno called the work of barbarians,
not artists.[9] In fact, the very confusion attendant upon the
chivalric kind of plot in the trackless forest is a means of
keeping fantasy alive and creating imagery of a spontaneous
wonder.

In a romance, adventures along the way will necessarily
first present themselves as visual experiences; their essence is
that they are unforeseen and that therefore the knight-errant
meets something visually arresting before he has any understanding of its significance for him. Guyon, for example, did
not know who Mammon was when he first "found in secret
shade / An uncouth, salvage, and uncivile wight, / Of griesly
hew and fowle ill-favour'd sight." And so the poet has ample
opportunity for description, without running the risk of having a succession of set pieces that might seem designed only

to display his own skill in making *ekphrases.* The plot justifies the predominance of pictorial imagery because it is conceived primarily as visual experiences requiring interpretation and subsequent action.

All this belongs to the genre Spenser chose, but this genre also committed him to a certain style by which the whole ready-made world of medieval romance might be evoked by means of formulaic expressions. These expressions encourage the reader to respond to something already familiar as a type of fiction and to complete in his own mind the pictures adumbrated by the poet.[10] He does not have to be extremely detailed—in fact, too much detail would disturb the whole process of imagining what the poet only alludes to.

But Spenser's use of the formulas of medieval romance has, as well, another aspect which can seem to run counter to the very freedom of fantasy that I have been emphasizing. This other aspect is the danger implicit in a poet's use of stereotypes: he may fail to endow them with new life, as happens occasionally in *The Faerie Queene.* When fantasy turns to clichés, it loses its power of enthrallment and leaves truth itself on the level of platitude. One might cite the battle scenes as an example of what the genre requires but what does not engage the poet's imagination.[11] Spenser is left to make the best he can of these by giving them decorative value: purple drops of blood contrasting with snowy skin or with green grass. Beyond such color contrasts, his effort to turn the melee of battle, with its shivered spears and tumbled heaps of bodies, into a work of art suggests a parallel with quattrocento painting, manuscript illuminations, and tapestries. In both *The Faerie Queene* and in these visual representations, it is the pageantry of warfare that dominates the portrayal. Perhaps the trappings of chivalry had something to do with encouraging people to embrace the idea of death and destruction; perhaps, too, a decorative archaism meant that only within certain stylistic conventions could violence be portrayed.

At any rate, so orderly is the universe of Spenser's poem that confusion itself has its place within the pattern. There is room for fire-breathing dragons, just as there is room for all the beasts whose aggressive behavior furnishes parallels, in the form of epic similes, to the knightly combats. We see a bull beset by two mastiffs, or two starving tigers battling over "some beasts fresh spoyle," or a gryphon defending its prey from a dragon. These beasts recall Spenser's interest in actual heraldry, when, for example, he pauses to describe a stranger knight's coat of arms as "a lion passant in a golden field." Not only does he love the decorative detail enough to give his final alexandrine to it but he also tends to turn all violent action into pattern, so that it becomes something like the device of the knight Sanglier: "A broken sword within a bloodie field." Finally, the stylization of Spenser's battle scenes is a reminder that whenever he is at a loss for imaginative and emotional response to the counters of romance, he will, as artist, always fall back upon pattern and symmetry to carry him through.

II

If the battles of *The Faerie Queene* testify to Spenser's sense of decorum, there are other signs that in planning his poem he was preoccupied with the claims of his genre. In the hierarchy of the genres, epic certainly held first place but romance might qualify both as a modern development of epic and as a popular form for the age Spenser was writing in. His poem is really an attempt to meet conflicting demands: the demand for unity and the demand for variety; for pleasure and for teaching; for the traditions of the classics and the innovations of the moderns. Yet in Books III and IV, we may find, if we

are so inclined, evidence of a capitulation to the popular appeal of romance, for these books do not have the formal
order to make them units in a whole made up of independent
parts. Was Spenser blundering, unable to revise in accordance with his scheme, or was he seeking the more ignorant
audience which demands, not the rational pleasures of symmetry and order, but the sensual pleasures of variety and
fantasy? Even if these books were written earlier and were
adapted to the scheme, instead of being written with the
scheme in mind,[12] they do conform to the tastes of the moderns, to nature rather than the rules, to the ignorant rather
than the learned. Adopting throughout the poem not only
variety of incident but also the canto division with its nonschematic form and a discursive style of narrative, Spenser
made the concessions necessary to win his audience.

But he could not be satisfied artistically or morally with
romance unless it was rationalized. It was not enough for him
to choose an Arthurian fairyland as his milieu; he also needed
to dispose his material according to formal principles. Romance, as Rosemond Tuve has admirably demonstrated, does
indeed lend itself to allegory in that the unknown constantly
beckons on every level, and therefore everything invites interpretation in terms of an overruling moral order.[13] But this
order finds its confirmation in the poem through the schematic structure to which Spenser aspired—witness his letter—even if he did not always attain it.

The "embodiment of an intention" is an apt definition of
poetic invention in the Renaissance. Although the schema
Spenser uses is not to be identified with his meaning, it must
be considered part of the method by which he conveys his
intention. Probably the sheer volume of his materials caused
him difficulty and uncertainty about the best arrangement,
but, at least when he wrote the letter, he believed in a "multiple unity," based on symmetry of the parts, with one hero

representing one of the twelve virtues in each book. Instead
of calling this type of order inorganic or mechanistic, it would
be better to avoid the pejorative connotations of these words
and call it an architectonic order. The use of architectural
analogies in Italian Renaissance criticism of such poets as
Dante, Ariosto, and Tasso is summed up in Tasso's remark
that "the poet must compose things together in a proper way,
according to necessity and according to verisimilitude, and
give them an appropriate form in the same way that the
architect customarily gives it to the stones with which he
builds."[14] Perhaps writers, as well as painters, "conceived
everything *sub specie architecturae*" because they too aspired
to a balancing of opposing forces or tensions to create the
most stable and exalted repose. Chastel refers to the "peculiar joys of architectonic calculation" which Alberti describes
in *Della tranquillità dell'animo*: "the mental construction of
exact systems, the elements of which are linked in an orderly
fashion."[15] If the poem was to be analogous to the cosmos, a
true "world of glass," it must be ordered on the rational principle which Ficino sees as operating in the universe: "Therefore, we conclude that all things are led by one certain
orderer who is most full of reason."[16] Underlying Spenser's
concern with the symmetrical disposition of his material lay
this assumption that creation itself proceeded by the imposition of restrictive form. A Renaissance artist liked defined
limits, such as the mirror which frames whatever it reflects;
he liked, too, the closed form of his paintings and of his cosmos. Form must be given definition in the interests of intel-
ligibility, and it could be defined only in relationship to a
boundary.

Whatever the exact origins of Spenser's scheme of the
virtues, it is necessarily an arbitrary one. Why should there
be twelve virtues any more than seven? Various answers have
been proposed, ranging from the twelve virtues extracted

from Aristotle by medieval and Renaissance commentators to the number twelve in its association with epic tradition. But in any case, this number is certainly Spenser's architectonic choice, rather than a necessity of the material. And however many books of *The Faerie Queene* we had, the schematic plan would bring us no nearer to the "final unity" of Spenser's work;[17] arbitrary or restrictive form imposes an architectural unity, a deliberate delimitation of space, not a natural or necessary conclusion. There are no mysteries of form to be revealed in subsequent books: each follows the same fundamental pattern of the quest; each uses the interlace technique of romance. The reaching of the court of Gloriana could, in fact, do no more than provide a formal conclusion to a work with no inevitable conclusion.

Now it so happens that the only kind of order which will not interfere with the apparent freedom of fantasy is precisely external structure or restrictive form. Spenser's schematic plan for his poem imposes a rational order while leaving fantasy free because it provides only for an arrangement of materials, setting limits to each book, using parallels of various kinds, and generally aiming at symmetry of the parts of his poem. The largest use of parallel structure is to present a titular knight and his quest in each book, but the scheme of the virtues implies above all that virtues and vices will be lined up, facing each other in a way that unallegorical fiction is usually loth to permit. There is a regular use of paralleling within books, such as Una and Duessa, and between books, such as the good hills that appear in Books I, III, and VI. Even Spenser's gesture in the direction of traditional epic unity in the shape of Prince Arthur emphasizes parallel structure by causing him to appear in the eighth canto of almost every book. Like the annual feast mentioned in the prefatory letter, Arthur is an element of external structure, and if we can accept that kind of boundary for the poem, we should be able to accept the way the prince helps to articulate the rational structure, which is like a grid placed over the dreamlike manifestations of a mysterious world.

Throughout the poem, schematic form supplies frames within which fantasy can express itself. The stanza acts restrictively, limiting descriptions to its dimensions, emphasizing them by framing them and, in short, acting as the cell to contain the honey. Yet for the sake of the journey and the story, stanza connections are stressed by conjunctions such as *and, but, wherefore,* as well as by repetitions of words and other kinds of transitions. Although progress toward the goal cannot in the nature of things be direct but rather through the labyrinths of forest and experience, the retarding movement of description never really stops the compulsion to keep going. Thus the two impulses—to pause and to proceed—are held in balance. A similar concern for continuity leads Spenser to make the books of his poem overlap, as well as to maintain their place as self-contained units in the whole poem.[18] For another reason too, sequence matters: the parts must be related to a whole which can only be realized in time. Whether one sees a sequence from three personal virtues to three social virtues, or whether one sees a more complex triadic plan, it seems clear that Spenser was trying to fit his units into an architectural scheme that would be both rational and harmonious, like Michelangelo's Sistine Chapel ceiling, where similarly both parallelism and sequence are emphasized by painted architectural frames. If Spenser's is an incomplete building, it is more truly so than Chaucer's *Canterbury Tales* because a rational design is presupposed in which completeness is an artistic necessity as it was not for Chaucer's more casual plan.

Yet perhaps the incompleteness of Spenser's poem is symbolically right, however far short it falls of his dream of formal perfection. After all, each of the books he did write leaves some sense of incompleteness, in order to show how there can be no finality here below until "that same time when no more change shall be." His stanzas end, not on a strong conclusive note, but on the lingering alexandrine, as though to make us muse on the passing scene. Everything suggests that Spenser was careful not to let his imposed formal limits inhibit the expressiveness of fantasy but rather to leave a slight gap for the infinite to come through.

These two kinds of form—expressive and restrictive—in their complex relationships have a decisive effect on the imagery of *The Faerie Queene.* When Spenser chose romance as his essential genre, he allowed himself a descriptive expansiveness, a dreaminess, which was certain to affect even his most emblematic images. Such figures as Duessa and Pyrochles come from the pages of emblem books into a story in which their salient features of false beauty and burning rage take on a childlike wonder for the reader. In the following description of Pyrochles, it may be observed how an image which grows out of an action and takes part in it possesses more life, color, and motion than a static emblem could:

After that varlets flight, it was not long,
Ere on the plaine fast pricking Guyon spide
One in bright armes embatteiled full strong,
That as the sunny beames doe glaunce and glide
Upon the trembling wave, so shined bright,
And round about him threw forth sparkling fire,
That seemd him to enflame on every side:
His steed was bloody red, and fomed yre,
When with the maistring spur he did him roughly stire.
(2.5.2)

Indeed, it is the poetic and narrative role of such images, in contrast with the more strictly meditative function of the emblem, which brings them into the realm of fantasy. In lan-

guage, or rather in high poetry, their mystery is created. Instead of being subordinated to didactic purpose, they have
become art, in which the ordinary didactic yields to the pursuit of an imaginative beauty which can teach more effectu-
ally by swaying the hearts of the readers. It is the same with
Mammon, who instead of being a mere figure of avarice takes
on the evocative qualities of a blacksmith god who is also a
haunted man.

At the same time, what occurs naturally in romance—figures of good and evil—is isolated and heightened to become
emblem, and what would be only obscurely significant becomes intellectually apprehensible as part of a coherent system of values. The very consciousness of symbolic meaning
on the part of the poet raises the individual romance image to
a new intensity as worthy of contemplation. In the Pyrochles
description, it may be noted that the figure has taken on a
perversely chivalric role, as indicated by the extreme brightness of his armor and the excessively foaming steed. When,
in addition, he is fitted to the stanza in such a way as to frame
him, he seems to fill our entire visual field. After two lines of
narrative introduction, the central part of the stanza is devoted to describing the brightness of the knight's arms, with
the help of a simile, "That as the sunny beames do glaunce
and glide / Upon the trembling wave," which suggests the
emotional turmoil beneath all this glitter. Finally, the last two
lines of the stanza focus on his blood-red steed and his goad-
ing of it, just as he goads himself to fury. The definition of the
image is directly related to its isolation within the stanza
scheme. Instead of stifling a fantasy image, restrictive order
can actually intensify its value, making it deserve its elabora-
tion into the nine-line stanza, even into the alexandrine, to
show that it is to be contemplated at length, however strong
the linear movement represented by the journey. And beyond the limits of the stanza, the image takes its place in a

book, which in turn fits into the whole scheme of the virtues. Like a series of Chinese boxes, the images, amazingly free in themselves, fit into larger structures based only partly on narrative continuity and more on the allegorical scheme of the poem.

In his balancing of the claims of fantasy with the claims of rational design, Spenser was answering in his own way the criticism of his friend Gabriel Harvey, who feared lest in *The Faerie Queene* Hobgoblin might "runne away with the garland from Apollo."[19] Sometimes, indeed, we may feel that there is too much order, too much symmetry, or that stylization has substituted for the liveliness of the image. But these are simply aspects of the impulse toward order which governs the whole of *The Faerie Queene* and which relates the images to the larger patterns of a universe which itself came into being through "the ornament of forms."[20]

NOTES

1. On the cooperation of reason and imagination in invention, see my article "Allegory as a Form of Wit," *Studies in the Renaissance,* 11 (1964), 225–33.

2. George Puttenham, *The Arte of English Poesie* (1589), ed. G. D. Willcock and A. Walker (Cambridge, 1936), pp. 19–20.

3. Epistle to Gabriel Harvey, prefixed to *The Shepheardes Calender.*

4. Rosemond Tuve's definition of "invention" in her *Reading of George Herbert* (Chicago, 1952), p. 188.

5. On the virtues and vices as commonplaces in Renaissance education and thought, see Joan Marie Lechner, *Renaissance Concepts of the Commonplaces* (New York, 1962), pp. 201–25.

6. See, for example, Tasso, *Discourses on the Heroic Poem,* trans. and ed. Mariella Cavalchini and Irene Samuel (Oxford,

1973), p. 32. See also the discussion in Hathaway, *Age of Criticism,* p. 395.

7. John Hughes, *An Essay on Allegorical Poetry,* in his edition of Spenser's *Works* (1715), I.xxv–lvii; reprinted in R. M. Cummings, *Spenser: The Critical Heritage* (New York, 1971), p. 261.

8. See C. S. Lewis, "Edmund Spenser," in *Major British Writers* (New York, 1954), 1:97–98, and Rosemond Tuve, *Allegorical Imagery* (Princeton, 1966), ch. 5. Cf. Giraldi Cinthio, *On Romances* (1554), trans. Henry L. Suggs (Lexington, 1968), pp. 37–39.

9. Minturno, *L'Arte Poetica,* selections in A. H. Gilbert, *Literary Criticism: Plato to Dryden* (1940; rpt. Detroit, 1962), pp. 284–85.

10. Cf. Michael Baxandall, *Painting and Experience in Fifteenth Century Italy* (Oxford, 1972), p. 46. Baxandall explains that the fifteenth-century painter did not try "to give detailed characterizations of people and places: it would have been an interference with the individual's private visualization if he had."

11. C. S. Lewis in *The Allegory of Love* (Oxford, 1936), p. 347, refers to Spenser's "big, set battle-pieces" as the kind of thing that he does "very badly."

12. See Josephine Waters Bennett, *The Evolution of the Faerie Queene* (Chicago, 1942).

13. Tuve, *Allegorical Imagery.*

14. Cited in Bernard Weinberg, *A History of Literary Criticism in the Italian Renaissance* (Chicago, 1961), 2:1030.

15. André Chastel, *The Age of Humanism,* trans. K. M. Delavenay and E. M. Gwyer (London, 1963), p. 218.

16. Marsilio Ficino, "Concerning the Mind," in *The Renaissance Philosophy of Man,* ed. E. Cassirer, P. O. Kristeller, and J. H. Randall (Chicago, 1948), p. 195.

17. Kathleen Williams expresses the opposite view. See her essay " 'Eterne in Mutabilitie': The Unified World of *The Faerie Queene,*" in *That Soueraine Light,* ed. W. R. Mueller and D. C. Allen (Baltimore, 1952), p. 35.

18. As already indicated, the canto divisions are nonschematic and really slices of the narrative, following the tradition of oral recitation, used for example by Ariosto. On the onward movement of the narrative, cf. C. S. Lewis's reference to Spenser's "business-like progression" (*English Literature in the Sixteenth Century* [Oxford, 1954], p. 389).

19. *The Works of Edmund Spenser, A Variorum Edition. The Prose Works,* ed. Rudolf Gottfried (Baltimore, 1949), p. 472.

20. Ficino, *Commentary on Plato's Symposium,* p. 129.

CHAPTER 2

"So Lively and So Like":
The Pursuit of Illusion

I

When Spenser refers to his poem as a mirror, he has in mind both its illusionistic quality and its truth-revealing purpose. He paints pictures because he accepts the general Renaissance view that art should imitate nature, and, in telling a story, he seeks the liveliness of experience. Through his imagination he brings to life the clichés or formulas of the romance tradition. At the same time, the transformation of romance motifs into a new, living reality owes much to the allegorical significance he bestows upon them. Here is not only the renewal of the old but the artistic sophistication of a naive genre.

The first reference to *The Faerie Queene* as a mirror occurs in the Proem to Book II, where Spenser addresses the queen:

> And thou, O fayrest Princesse under sky,
> In this fayre mirrhour maist behold thy face,
> And thine owne realmes in lond of Faery,
> And in this antique ymage thy great auncestry.
> (2.Proem.4)

34

It sounds like the familiar advice to princes—a courtesy book for the court to learn from. The next mirror reference, in Book III, also tells the queen to see herself in figures of the poem:

Ne let his fayrest Cynthia refuse,
In mirrours more then one her selfe to see,
But either Gloriana let her chuse,
Or in Belphoebe fashioned to bee:
In th' one her rule, in th' other her rare chastitee.

(3.Proem.5)

The implication that this is a true mirror recalls, in turn, Spenser's lines in *An Hymne of Heavenly Beautie,* where the divine virtues are said to appear in "th' image of his grace, / As in a looking glasse." For this is the only way "we fraile wights, whose sight cannot sustaine / The suns bright beames" can see "with feeble eyne / The glory of that Majestie Divine." Having grown up in this Platonic school, he knows how to treat all images as transparent metaphors.

For Spenser, as for Shakespeare and Cervantes, the greater art's mastery of illusion, the more the illusory nature of reality comes to the fore. Like Plato, he seems to be saying, "For there is no light of justice or temperance or any of the higher ideas which are precious to souls in the earthly copies of them; they are seen through a glass dimly; and there are few who, going to the images, behold in them the realities, and these only with difficulty."[1] The mirror is thus a potentially unreliable source of knowledge in that what it shows is transient and unsubstantial. It is altogether illusion and may deceive, as false courtesy certainly does:

Fashion'd to please the eies of them that pas,
Which see not perfect things but in a glas:
Yet is that glasse so gay that it can blynd
The wisest sight, to thinke golde that is bras.

(6.Proem.5)

Yet when Spenser chose fairyland as his symbolic medium, he was deliberately choosing, not a realm where judgment has already occurred, such as Dante's afterlife, but, instead, a place where uncertainty prevails and where the world of appearances is the testing ground of the soul. He is calling upon illusion to act as a critique of illusion, revealing the fallacies of sight and the need for insight.

This is why he invokes the Muse as he does, in order that he may make a true mirror of the virtues:

> Revele to me the sacred noursery
> Of Vertue, which with you doth there remaine,
> Where it in silver bowre does hidden ly.
>
> (6.Proem.3)

The "silver bowre" echoes "the moon's fair shining sphere" of the Proem to Book II. However expository the design of *The Faerie Queene,* the imagination at work offers no explanation but is receptive. It is not by chance that Spenser likes the adjective "inly" or that, like the moon, his poem catches the light, is not a source of light. If Shakespeare's genius is solar and masculine, Spenser's is lunar and feminine. But as a medium for the divine, he is something more than a didactic poet; he dwells on the inwardness of his vision:

> But Vertues seat is deepe within the mynd,
> And not in outward shows, but inward thoughts defynd.
>
> (6.Proem.5)

As for his poem, his hopes for it inevitably remind us of his description of Merlin's magic mirror, the "world of glass":

> It vertue had to shew in perfect sight
> What ever thing was in the world contaynd,
> Betwixt the lowest earth and hevens hight,
> So that it to the looker appertaynd.
>
> (3.2.19)

In like fashion Spenser gives a picture of everything "Betwixt the lowest earth and hevens hight, / So that it to the looker appertaynd"—as it must appertain if his allegory is grasped at all; and there is a level on which even a child can grasp it.

The Spenser of *The Faerie Queene* is, then, primarily a mythological poet, appealing to fantasy in somewhat the sense in which Tasso uses that word, invoking its etymology of "light-bearing."[2] The images of romance, in all their descriptive amplitude, are shaped with a new purpose as a lesson in aesthetic discrimination. But unless we grant the spellbinding quality of Spenser's story, its appeal to the reader's fantasy, we have lost a good part of the light. As Puttenham describes fantasy, it acts like a true or false mirror:

> And this phantasie may be resembled to a glasse as hath beene sayd, whereof there be many tempers and manner of makinges, as the perspectiues doe acknowledge, for some be false glasses and shew thinges otherwise than they be in deede, and others right as they be in deede, neither fairer nor fouler, nor greater nor smaller. There be againe of these glasses that shew thinges exceeding faire and comely, others that shew figures very monstruous and illfauored. Even so is the phantasticall part of man (if it be not disordered) a representer of the best, most comely and bewtifull images or apparances of thinges to the soule and according to their very truth.[3]

We are reminded of Spenser's reference in the October eclogue to the beauty of Colin Clout's beloved as an "immortal mirrhor," because she is the concrete image through which a wiser Colin might perceive the nature of God; that is, if he were not so caught up in sensuous particulars as to lose sight of the eternal. The mirror image always seems to imply the particular through which the universal is apprehended. This surely is the sense in which Spenser uses the word. But in

The Faerie Queene, it is not the isolated image but the whole of the narrative which acts as a mirror to figure forth the truth.

II

Ut pictura poesis, the analogy between poetry and painting, implies that poetry shares with painting the same purpose of mirroring the world of real experience.[4] For painting certainly, the mirror was "the master of painters," so that this was not simply a theoretical analogy. Leonardo da Vinci is not alone in recommending that the painter use the mirror to check the verisimilitude of his work: "When you wish to see whether your painting altogether conforms with the thing drawn from nature, take a mirror and reflect the living thing in it. Compare the thing reflected with your picture and consider well whether the subject of both representations is in conformity in both cases."[5] This literal use of the word "mirror" in discussions of painting obviously has to give way to a metaphorical use when poetry is the subject. Hamlet can speak of a play as holding "the mirror up to nature" without any particular emphasis on the pictorial qualities of imagery; instead, the play as a whole constitutes the picture. Closer to Spenser's use of the word "mirror," however, is Ben Jonson's claim: "My mirror is more subtle, cleere, refin'd, / And takes and gives the beauties of the mind."[6] This is a typical Renaissance separation of the provinces of poetry and painting, with painting assigned the task of depicting the body, whereas poetry alone can depict the mind. This is not quite fair to either poet or painter, but it suggests how the *paragone,* the rivalry of the arts, might be turned to the poet's advantage, since the "beauties of the mind" matter more than those of the body.

If, then, the painter excels at representing the visible world, the poet excels at representing the invisible. This distinction, rather than Lessing's between the space-art of painting and the time-art of poetry, pervades Renaissance criticism, although poet and painter also aspire to steal some of the power of their rival artist, just as both attempt to steal from their still greater rival—nature herself. The very intransigence of the medium becomes any artist's spur to the highest achievement. The poet will attempt—notwithstanding Lessing's strictures—to make bodies visible, just as the painter will attempt to make his bodies express the spirit that animates them. In Sidney's words, the poet's task is like that of the excellent painter who, in depicting Lucretia "whom he never saw," would paint "the outward beauty of such a virtue."[7] That is to say, the true poet will have his gaze fixed on the beauty of the ideal, for which he must fashion a fitting mirror.

But for poetry to become such a mirror, the reader's imagination must become a participant in the creation, as Shakespeare was to say in his Prologue to *Henry V:*

> Think, when we talk of horses, that you see them,
> Printing their proud hoofs i' th' receiving earth.
>
> (ll. 26–27)

His *Rape of Lucrece* similarly comments on the role of the spectator in bringing a wall painting to life:

> For much imaginary work was there,—
> Conceit deceitful, so compact, so kind,
> That for Achilles' image stood his spear
> Grip'd in an armed hand, himself behind
> Was left unseen, save to the eye of mind:
> A hand, a foot, a face, a leg, a head
> Stood for the whole to be imagined.[8]
>
> (ll. 1422–28)

In poetry, it is for the reader to turn the words into picture, as the good viewer of painting will turn that into poetry. In

Leonardo's version of *ut pictura poesis,* "Painting is poetry which is seen and not heard, and poetry is a painting which is heard but not seen. These two arts, you may call them both either poetry or painting, have here interchanged the senses by which they penetrate to the intellect."[9]

In achieving fullness of effect, however, pictures seemed to have a natural advantage, and Leonardo has little difficulty building up a case for the superior power of the painted image as distinct from the verbal: in particular, painting uses natural signs immediately recognizable to anyone (a faith no longer held with such certainty today, thanks to studies in visual perception), whereas poetry uses artificial means, words which bear no relationship to the reality they are imitating. But the tables might seem to be turned when the debate centers on allegory, as it does in a passage in Shakespeare's *Timon of Athens.* Now the poet is sure that he has the advantage, only to be reminded by the painter, "A thousand moral paintings I can show" (I.i.90). There is no such thing as a clear winner in these debates over the relative merits of the arts.

One might indeed wonder why there was such persistent, widespread interest in the rivalry of the arts, which, although related to the social positions of the various practitioners, seems to take a philosophical form, as if it contained the possibility of answering some ultimate question. What is certain is that each of the arts felt the necessity of transcending its own limitations, or as Leonardo in speaking of poetry and painting put it: they have "interchanged the senses by which they penetrate to the intellect." Is this not virtually a definition of metaphor? I would suggest that it is just this sense of the metaphorical function of any medium that is at the heart of the Renaissance comparison of the arts.

As we might expect, it is a poet who most clearly recognizes the metaphorical value of the expression *ut pictura poesis.* Sir Philip Sidney, following Aristotle, defines poetry as an art of imitation, "that is to say, a representing, counterfeiting, or figuring forth—to speak metaphorically, a speaking picture." In using the phrase "to speak metaphorically" as a safeguard against possible misinterpretation of *ut pictura poesis,* he shows his awareness that the real enemies of poetry are the literalists. He then goes on to distinguish graphically between illusion and deception. Using the theater as a classic instance of illusion, he asks, "What child is there that, coming to a play, and seeing *Thebes* written in great letters upon an old door, doth believe that it is Thebes? If then a man can arrive, at that child's age, to know that the poets' persons and doings are but pictures what should be, and not stories what have been, they will never give the lie to things not affirmatively but allegorically and figuratively written."[10] So Sidney has placed us, or tried to place us, in a frame of mind for acquiescing in the metaphorical properties of the specific kind of illusion created in poetry. But he must have been aware that the illusion created in painting could equally be condemned as a form of lying. In Sir Edward Hoby's 1586 translation of Coignet's *Politique Discourses,* for example, painting and poetry are classed together as both yielding "pleasure by lying."[11] In view of the usual Platonically inspired moral judgment on illusion, Sidney was clearly justified in spelling out the difference between illusion and deception and emphasizing the metaphor in the matter.

But the proper context for interpreting *ut pictura poesis* can only be the whole aesthetic which required that every art interchange with another art the sense by which it penetrates to the intellect, to use the words of Leonardo. For if poetry is a speaking picture and painting a dumb poetry, one art has in effect become another. So pervasive a concept can here be illustrated only at random. Alberti, for example, praises in painting "those faces which, as though carved, appear to issue out of the panel."[12] All the decorative arts were expected to mimic the effects of another medium than the one in which they were formed; it is with pride that Sabbia di Castiglione in his description of the ways to decorate a house mentions his "little figure of St. Jerome, in clay but imitating bronze." For the same kind of virtuosity he praises the intarsia work of Fra Damiano da Bergamo, who "not only in perspective views . . . but in landscape, in pictures of houses, in distant views, and, what is more, in figures, can do with wood all that the great Apelles could hardly do with the brush. In fact," he continues, "it seems to me that the colors of those woods are more vivid, brighter, and more agreeable than those used by painters, so that these noble works can be called a new sort of painting, excellently painted without paints."[13] If intarsia attempted to master the same field as painting, it was only one among the many forms of Renaissance decorative art with this aim. One thinks of Ghiberti's illusionism in bronze, or of embroidery which has such invisible stitches that it looks more like painting. Indeed, it may appear that all the arts of this time aspired to the condition of painting. No higher praise of Dürer's engravings can be given than to say, with Dolce, that "his figures seem not only designed, but painted; and not painted only, but to live."[14] But this is the point: painting is singled out as the ultimate example of illusionist art. It was even ordained that music by its exact, almost word by word, illustration of a text should eloquently paint the emotions.

Of particular relevance here is the rhetorical display piece called *ekphrasis*. Rhetorical tradition had given a good deal of attention to the means of bringing places, persons, and works of art vividly before a reader's or listener's eyes, and the technique was not lost on poets who had a similar aim, especially narrative poets. As George Puttenham wrote in 1589, "in that which the Poet speakes or reports of another mans tale or doings, as *Homer* of *Priamus* or *Vlisses,* he is as the painter or keruer that worke by imitation and representation in a forrein subject."[15] The example he gives of a "forrein subject"—"a liuely purtraite," in a painter's or carver's "table of wood"—makes it clear that he has in mind the difference between the medium and the subject represented. But once again, what matters to these critics is the artist's ability to transcend his medium. Just as paint should do the impossible in realistic representation, so words by the poet's Orphic charm must lose their verbality to become painting. A favorite Renaissance instance of the poet's success is summed up in Cicero's praise of Homer: "It is reported that Homer was blind. But we see that he has given us a picture rather than a poem. What country, what shores, what place in Greece, what kind of form, what battles, what armies, what rowing of a ship, what motion of men or of wild beasts— which of these has he not so painted that what he did not see himself he has made us to see?"[16] When everything is thus brought before the eyes of the reader, poetry possesses that *enargeia* or efficacy which Cicero and Quintilian brought to the notice of Renaissance critics.

If poetry is praised in terms of picture, it is to be expected that painting should be praised as narrative. Here again the rhetorical treatment of *ekphrasis* encouraged a traditional mode of panegyric. From Philostratus to Vasari,[17] the descent is clear: the dumb poetry of painting finds its voice. One cannot but wonder at the long history of this convention, at the once-fashionable desire of writers to pay tribute to their sister art by praising its power to tell a story, just as literature was once praised for its ability to bring pictures before the mind's eye. When Vasari praises Homer for describing Achilles's shield "with such art that we seem to see it carved and painted before our eyes rather than merely described,"[18] his view may be compared with Homer's own admiration for the skill of the craftsman who could represent in gold the dark furrows of the new-ploughed field. It has never crossed the minds of either that it is the duty of the artist to observe the limits of his medium. On the contrary, they assume that the artist wishes to demonstrate his godlike power by improving on the imperfection of his material. It is this triumph that *ekphrasis* is designed to praise, but in so doing, it aspires to a similar end: conquest of its own verbal medium.

But perhaps the most extraordinary aspect of the merging of media during the Renaissance lies in treating art and nature as if they were rival media, each struggling to emulate the other.[19] As we have seen, the perfection of any art form was thought to consist in its taking on the expressive attributes of another medium. The whole quest for the achievement of illusion is, of course, an attempt to make art imitate nature; but the reverse — the habit of praising nature in terms of art — also holds sway in all Renaissance literature. Some of Shakespeare's loveliest lines do just this, whether it is the description of the moon in *A Midsummer Night's Dream* as "like to a silver bow / New-bent in heaven" (I.i.9–10), or of the stars in *The Merchant of Venice* as making "the floor of heaven" look "thick inlaid with patens of bright gold" (V.i.58–59). Yet this ornamental conception of nature pervades, too, the description of people. Spenser, wishing to convey the beautiful sight of the Graces dancing around Colin Clout's beloved, cannot find a better image than that of a precious stone set in a ring:

> And in the middest of those same three was placed
> Another damzell, as a precious gemme
> Amidst a ring most richly well enchaced.
>
> (6.10.12)

In equally decorative terms, the blush on a maiden's cheek is described:

And ever and anone with rosie red
The bashfull blood her snowy cheekes did dye,
That her became, as polisht yvory
Which cunning craftesman hand hath overlayd
With fayre vermilion or pure castory.

(2.9.41)

If illusion is the end of art, it is also true that ornament is the end of nature. Neither one can be seen without reference to the other: art and nature aspire to interchange their terms. Here we have the most all-inclusive instance of metaphorical thinking about the medium of expression. For nature is itself the medium of God's expression, according to the favorite Renaissance topos used by such writers as Castiglione and Vasari to praise art. But no medium, as they saw it, was capable of achieving expression solely in its own terms. To transcend the limitations of his medium was, therefore, the perpetual struggle of every artist, including God; the dialectic of life required no less.

This may, of course, be considered a mere display of virtuosity, an overcoming of difficulty,[20] but there are, I believe, other implications which we sometimes tend to lose sight of. It is refreshing to return to such a simple statement as the one Sir John Harington makes in his preface to his translation of Ariosto. In drawing attention to the relationship of the engravings to the text, he says; "The vse of the Picture is euident, which is, that (hauing read ouer the booke) you may reade it (as it were againe) in the very picture."[21] Now it is easy to say that he is only expressing the emblematic habit of mind, but that statement tells us nothing about the habit of mind which could lead Harington to wish to establish a relationship between the picture and the text. He is really asking to have the same story read in two different media. But why bother? The only possible reason is that though the story is the same, it receives a different coloring from the difference in the medium.

Surely behind all the Renaissance interest in imitation lies some notion that the medium itself alters the sense of the imitation, that the imitation alludes to the object but is not the object. In art, where utility is not the primary value, there is no such thing as a simple replica. Even a bronze cast of an actual lizard or fly, as we see them on the Baldacchino in St. Peter's, is not merely a cast of dead life but living art. This allusive, and elusive, quality, this saying of one thing in terms of another, is a reminder that the virtuosity which the *paragone* seems to demand is not the whole story in the artist's triumph over his medium; conceivably, he may be forging a new metaphor, one which will show the subject with "more light and better note," to use the words of a sixteenth-century rhetorical definition of metaphor.[22]

III

Spenser's own mirrorlike art cannot, obviously, be compared with the bronze cast of a lizard or a fly, any more than a sonneteer's claim to be painting the portrait of his lady can be taken literally. In fact, his own criticism of the visual arts almost seems to turn upon their illusionistic power. In this, he conforms to the Platonic tradition, as it continues in St. Augustine and in Ficino and even in Protestantism, according to which the visual arts must always be on a lower scale than poetry because their appeal is so much more related to sensation than is the appeal of poetry, which is entirely of the mind and presumed to be more rational in its purpose.[23] Like other Renaissance writers, Spenser chooses to use the terms of the *paragone,* the rivalry between poetry and painting, as a way of speaking about how the artist presents truth.

In effect, he goes beyond recognizing illusion as the chief goal of both poetry and painting by insisting that art must be judged not only by the craftsman's skill but also by what the work of art represents. Remote as this emphasis on subject matter is from the dominant view in modern art criticism, it needs to be examined in some detail. Consider, for example, the four statues described in *The Faerie Queene.* They are not, strictly speaking, art: they are cult figures. Nevertheless, beauty is irrelevant to only one of them—the idol put up by Geryoneo in the form of his father (5.11). Both father and son, we are told, combine "three bodies powre" in one, and power seems implied in the description of this statue as "of massy gold / Most richly made." There is no sign of the monster hidden beneath the altar. Not until Prince Arthur strikes the idol three times with his sword does it emerge to do battle; but the rich workmanship used to represent Geryoneo's "owne vaine fancies thought" must not be allowed to conceal the repulsive creature beneath. The unmasking of evil, not the admiration of art, is what ultimately concerns the hero.

The other three statues are more problematic, as well as more interesting in their details. The statue of Cupid in the House of Busirane is also "Of massy gold," but it differs from Geryoneo's idol in appearing to be beautiful. It shines with its "owne light"—false though this light is—and its wings are "with sondry colours dight / More sondry colours then the proud pavone / Beares in his boasted fan, or Iris bright, / When her discolourd bow she spreds through hevens hight" (3.11.47). Now the apparent beauty of art helps to promote "fowle idolatree," and even for Britomart "the passing brightnes her fraile sences dazd."[24] It is only in a world which reveres the beauty of craftsmanship as much as Spenser's does that art possesses the power to corrupt.

The statues of Isis and Venus, however, show beauty put to better purpose. The one of Isis, "with fayned colours shading a true case," impels Britomart to prostrate herself before it. This idol "formed all of silver fine / So well as could with cunning hand be wrought" represents "that part of justice which is equity"; hence she may be called "goddess" without "fowle idolatree." Her dress in its rich simplicity confirms her mystery:

> And clothed all in garments made of line,
> Hemd all about with fringe of silver twine.
> Uppon her head she wore a crowne of gold,
> To shew that she had powre in things divine.
>
> (5.7.6)

So used, art does not express a "vaine fancies thought" but fittingly reminds the viewer of the need for reverence before the mystery of divine law.[25]

But the most detailed of Spenser's statue descriptions is the one of Venus, perhaps because she is "great Beauties Queene" (*HB*.267), whom Spenser himself worships. A mystery is implied in the very construction of the statue, as if it were not the work of mortal hands, yet could scarcely be depicted except by analogy with human craftsmanship. First, the substance is "uneath to understand":

> For neither pretious stone, nor durefull brasse,
> Nor shining gold, nor mouldring clay it was;
> But much more rare and pretious to esteeme,
> Pure in aspect, and like to christall glasse,
> Yet glasse was not, if one did rightly deeme,
> But being faire and brickle, likest glasse did seeme.
>
> (4.10.39)

What we are given to understand is that this is the most perfect representation of Venus ever fashioned:

But it in shape and beautie did excell
All other idoles which the heathen adore,
Farre passing that which by surpassing skill
Phidias did make in Paphos isle of yore.

But, as with the substance, the form is mysterious, being covered "with a slender veile afore" to conceal what the common people could not understand: her bisexual nature. Like the other three statues, this one also has a beast at the foot; here a snake "whose head and tail were fast combyned." These beasts seem to manifest the latent power of the idols; for power they all have, whether for good or for evil. They are the clearest evidence for Spenser's apparent conviction that art is not superfluous adornment but a force affecting how man lives. He might have agreed with Tasso's view that even if idols do not possess power in themselves, they do for "those wretches who . . . worshipped not the artificer but the artifice, not the sculptor but the statue."[26] The story of the youth who perished for love of a statue of Venus, alluded to in this passage, is only a conspicuous example of the idolatry to which art gives rise when its metaphorical nature is not clearly understood.[27]

A similar idolatry appears in Spenser's treatment of the False Florimell. In the *paragone* of art with nature, the artificial Florimell excels, created by a witch who is a master craftsman:

She there deviz'd a wondrous worke to frame,
Whose like on earth was never framed yit,
That even Nature selfe envide the same,
And grudg'd to see the counterfet should shame
The thing it selfe.   (3.8.5)

Like the lady framed by Archimago to deceive Red Cross, it is "so lively and so like" "That weaker sence it could have ravisht quight" (1.1.45). The False Florimell is also referred to as an "idole faire" (3.8.11) and, like the statues which Spenser calls idols, it serves as an object of worship. Even so, representational art, the art that rivals nature, invites the sin of Pygmalion—falling in love with an image. In the case of the False Florimell, the loss of metaphoric dimension is tellingly signaled by the literalization of the very metaphor Spenser had already used to describe the wonder of human eyes:

> Two goodly beacons, set in watches stead,
> Therein gave light, and flamd continually;
> For they of living fire most subtilly
> Were made, and set in silver sockets bright.
>
> (2.9.46)

Here, in the Castle of Alma, the metaphor of the "two goodly Beacons" enhances the wonder of divine workmanship; the witch's mechanical creation, on the other hand, actually has, in place of eyes, "two burning lamps" set "In silver sockets, shyning like the skies." The perfection of art thus turns to the perversion of nature: not only through the obvious intent to deceive but also through the wanton behavior of the substitute, so contrary to the chastity of the true Florimell. But when the two are placed side by side, nature triumphs over art:

> Then did he set her by that snowy one,
> Like the true saint beside the image set,
> Of their beauties to make paragone,
> And triall, whether should the honour get.
> Streight way so soone as both together met,
> Th' enchaunted damzell vanisht into nought:
> Her snowy substance melted as with heat,
> Ne of that goodly hew remayned ought,
> But th'emptie girdle, which about her wast was wrought.
>
> (5.3.24)

If nature is real, art is not; anything so dependent upon appearances as art is can last only so long as the viewer is under a spell. Just as the fine tapestries of the House of Busirane vanish with the overthrow of their magician, so the exposure of the Snowy Florimell to the truth of nature causes her to vanish.

Art as idol in fact gives the measure of its closeness to religion and magic. But even as decoration art may be dangerous, for, divorced from what is holy, it can shape man's native sensuality into more perverse forms than it would naturally give rise to, influencing him toward evil. Once again, we see that imitation, the emulative character of art, is the secret source of its power, and to this Spenser gives his special attention.

His most graphic treatment of this emulative character of art occurs in his poem *Muiopotmos,* in the form of the contest between Arachne and Minerva.[28] When Arachne challenged the goddess "to compare with her in curious skill / Of workes with loome, with needle, and with quill," Minerva "did the chalenge not refuse, / But deign'd with her the paragon to make." The competing tapestries are described in terms of lifelikeness: Arachne's depiction of Europa and the bull was "so lively seene, / That it true sea and true bull ye would weene" (ll. 279–80). But it is Minerva's embroidered butterfly that wins the contest:

> Emongst those leaves she made a butterflie,
> With excellent device and wondrous slight,
> Fluttring among the olives wantonly,
> That seem'd to live, so like it was in sight:
> The velvet nap which on his wings doth lie,
> The silken downe with which his backe is dight,
> His broad, outstretched hornes, his hayrie thies,
> His glorious colours, and his glistering eies.
>
> (ll. 329–36)

Arachne's reaction to "workmanship so rare" was to stand "astonied long, ne ought gainesaid." The rivals accept precisely the same standard of artistic excellence, and Minerva's tapestry is clearly the superior in the imitation of nature. But the differences of subject matter in the two competition pieces also imply a moral difference, and here too Minerva's is the superior. Arachne has chosen to represent "how Jove did abuse / Europa like a bull," a scene fittingly enclosed by "an yvie winding trayle." The wantonness of this work contrasts with Minerva's tapestry depicting her victory over Neptune in establishing Athens as a city of peace and good government, with her olive tree as the appropriate symbol. Even her embroidered butterfly triumphs not merely by craftsmanship; it is morally superior because it is the soul. Spenser, here as elsewhere, refuses to make fine workmanship the sole criterion for judging art, however much he may praise it.

When we turn to decorative art in particular settings, the moral significance of subject matter becomes even more apparent; now art must be judged by its decorum, which means not only its appropriateness to the setting but its purpose within that setting. This indeed is the ultimate criterion by which Spenser judges art. But on a lower level, he can praise the workman's skill in making the tapestries of Castle Joyous and the House of Busirane. Thus the Venus and Adonis tapestry is "A worke of rare device and wondrous wit," and in his own attempt to recreate it in words, he competes with the craftsman, who was also competing with Ovid. So poetry returns to poetry, but with a greater sensuality and richness, because, rather than describing events, Spenser is describing a piece of decoration, one appropriate to Castle Joyous. Instead of Ovid's emphasis on Venus's unusual hunting activities, Spenser gives a description of sensual indulgence, with Venus spreading "her mantle, colour'd like the starry skyes, /

And her soft arme lay underneath his hed"—with many more details in this vein, amid an atmosphere of secrecy and covert lust. Next to Spenser's account, Ovid's appears quite chaste. In this way, our poet has set the mood for Castle Joyous. The art object may be fully appropriate to the lustful setting but it also partakes of the same sin. Impeccable as craftsmanship, this "worke of rare device and wondrous wit" is vitiated as art in its higher sense, which implies a whole relationship to life.

Similarly, the mood of the House of Busirane is set by "goodly arras of great majesty." Again, the poet must praise the craftsmanship for its lifelikeness: "Ah! how the fearefull ladies tender hart / Did lively seeme to tremble, when she saw / The huge seas under her t'obay her servaunts law!" and again he notes the marvel of the invention: "wondrous skill and sweet wit of the man, / That her in daffadillies sleeping made." But at the beginning and end of the whole description, the word "long," used for the snakelike metal thread running through the tapestries and for the bloody river which serves as a border round the scenes, underlines both the insidiousness and the power of Cupid. These scenes are not presented for delight, like those alluded to in the Induction to *The Taming of the Shrew* or in Titian's "poesie" but, as the sheer number of the scenes implies, for far more sinister purpose.

Imitative art carries its own special responsibility for influencing the passions. But even the forms that do not imitate nature, like the "wilde anticks" of the third room, may so imitate fantasy images as to weaken reason. These "thousand monstrous forms" were made "in the rich metall, as they living were," and so they reinforce the spectator's perhaps latent impulses to surrender to the domination of the evil Cupid.

The Bower of Bliss also uses imitative art in order to sub-

vert reason. The *ekphrasis* of the ivory gate already sets the
theme of witchcraft and sensuality, yet Spenser praises the
craftsmanship as "a worke of admirable wit." With his own
rich imagination, he recreates not only the story but the
medium in which it is portrayed:

> Ye might have seene the frothy billowes fry
> Under the ship, as thorough them she went,
> That seemd the waves were into yvory,
> Or yvory into the waves were sent;
> And otherwhere the snowy substaunce sprent
> With vermell, like the boyes blood therein shed,
> A piteous spectacle did represent;
> And otherwhiles with gold besprinkeled,
> Yt seemd thenchaunted flame, which did Creusa wed.
>
> (2.12.45)

As in the tapestry descriptions, Spenser shows a connois-
seur's eye, but it is also the eye of a poet who imagined more
than he had actually seen and who gives the appreciative
viewer's response, in order to enable the reader in turn to
visualize what was there. These ivory waves contribute to a
total decorative scheme designed to seduce the eye which, as
Donne remarks in one of his sermons, is the Devil's door.[29]
Through the skill of the craftsman, the inert medium of ivory
is set in motion, and Spenser describes how the spectator's
view oscillates between awareness of the ivory substance and
the illusion of real waves: "That seemd the waves were into
yvory, / Or yvory into the waves were sent."[30] There is no
literal deception but, by drawing the spectator so subtly into
a story of uncontrollable passions, art has entered the service
of evil. It is Acrasia's metaphor, making her own statement
about the power of the evil Cupid.

In Spenser's descriptions of evil art, he emphasizes above
all the manipulation of the spectator. The golden grapes of
the Bower of Bliss oppress "the weake boughes" even as they

hide and emerge like the bathing damsels, who partly hid, partly revealed to Guyon's sight, "him more desirous made" (2.12.66). The golden ivy too is not only purposefully deceptive in its imitation of nature but dips "his lascivious armes" down into the fountain. The sin is not simply emulation of nature—how could it be with the Renaissance conviction that art should be lifelike?—but the too blatant insistence on the sensual message by exploiting all the resources of art.

Of these, one of the most compelling is a certain ambiguity which is inherent in artistic illusion, drawing the spectator into an imaginative participation, almost—as we have seen in the case of ivory waves on the gate of the Bower of Bliss—involving him in the very act of creation. But there is also an ambiguity in all our visual experience, which the artist in a sense is only exploiting: as Plato pointed out, we can even be deceived by the appearance of a stick of wood in water into thinking that the stick is bent. When Spenser describes the beauties of nature, he does not hesitate to show God himself as the creator of illusionistic effects, such as those of the River Medway:

> Then came the bride, the lovely Medua came,
> Clad in a vesture of unknowen geare,
> And uncouth fashion, yet her well became;
> That seem'd like silver, sprinckled here and theare
> With glittering spangs, that did like starres appeare,
> And wav'd upon, like water chamelot,
> To hide the metall, which yet every where
> Bewrayed it selfe, to let men plainely wot,
> It was no mortall worke, that seem'd and yet was not.
>
> (4.11.45)

The fascination and mystery of artistic illusion is suggested by the series of similes: "like silver," "like starres," "like water chamelot"—or watered silk. At the same time, the meta-

phorical silver thread of the river recalls the actual golden
thread of Busirane's tapestries that "lurked privily, / As faining to be hid from envious eye"; but in contrast to the cor-
rupting, snakelike art of the tapestries, the silver thread of
the Medway is innocent of everything but the beauty of illusion. Since no avaricious hands will ever rob this rich fabric of
its seeming metal, there is no need for titillating concealment.[31]

It is paradoxical, no doubt, that the art of God, like the art
of man, can only be described in terms of illusion, of "seeming." It is not only the golden ivy of the Bower that is so
colored "That wight who did not well avis'd it vew, / Would
surely deeme it to bee yvie trew"—it is also the River
Thames that has waves "So cunningly enwoven" that few
could "weenen whether they were false or trew" (4.11.27).
The ambiguity of all artistic illusion, both natural and man-
made, is an intrinsic part of its appeal, and Spenser has no
intention of dispensing with it in the interests of an oversim-
plified notion of truth. The line between good and evil art is
not so readily to be drawn. If both present an illusion, it is the
appropriateness, a higher sense of decorum, which alone can
sanctify art (or life, for that matter).

When art aids nature, it is really assisting a not-too-dissim-
ilar activity from its own, one that displays not only illusionistic effects but also decorative abundance. In the context of
pastoral idealism, however, nature's own skill suffices "to
worke delight" by creating a landscape of luxuriant but ordered beauty. Just as the Garden of Adonis needs no gar-
dener and has "a pleasant arber, not by art, / But of the trees
own inclination made," so in the seventh Mutability Canto,
Nature's pavilion is described as

>   Not such as craftes-men by their idle skill
>   Are wont for princes states to fashion:
>   But th' Earth her self, of her owne motion,

> Out of her fruitful bosome made to growe
> Most dainty trees, that, shooting up anon,
> Did seeme to bow their bloosming heads full lowe,
> For homage unto her, and like a throne did shew.
>   (7.7.8)

This apparent rejection of art's role in adorning princely courts is in keeping with the praise of idyllic nature in the pastoral episode of Book VI and the identification of virtue with an original state of innocence, so different from the "painted show" of worldly pleasures. No wonder the flowers "that voluntary grew" under Nature's feet seem richer "then any tapestry / That princes bowres adorne with painted imagery." Perhaps flowers in all their decorative appeal become the most significant test of the competing values of nature and art.

At the other extreme from Nature's realm are the flowers of the Bower of Bliss, and Spenser uses the metaphors of virgin and harlot to point the contrast between the two.[32] The lovely green grass of the Bower is "goodly beautifide"

> With all the ornaments of Floraes pride,
> Wherewith her mother Art, as halfe in scorne
> Of niggard Nature, like a pompous bride
> Did decke her, and too lavishly adorne,
> When forth from virgin bowre, she comes in th' early
>   morne.   (2.12.50)

Instead of assisting nature, art has entered into competition with her—"striving each th' other to undermine"—yet in their rivalry they merely succeed in making each other's work the more seductive to fallen man.

At the Temple of Venus, on the other hand, art supplies "what Nature did omit," as an act of friendship.[33] Now the lavishness of the flowers epitomizes the rightful pleasures of human sensuality:

No flowre in field, that daintie odour throwes,
And deckes his branch with blossomes over all,
But there was planted, or grew naturall:
Nor sense of man so coy and curious nice,
But there mote find to please it selfe withall;
Nor hart could wish for any queint device,
But there it present was, and did fraile sense entice.

(4.10.22)

Not even the final phrase has the connotations of evil which
it usually has; in this "second paradise" pleasure may freely
be allowed to reign. When art does indeed work hand in hand
with nature, it has the same function that nurture has in a
civilized society:

For all that Nature by her mother wit
Could frame in earth, and forme of substance base,
Was there, and all that Nature did omit,
Art, playing second Natures part, supplyed it.

(4.10.21)

In the Book of Friendship, it is fitting that art should play this
role. Perhaps the most telling detail concerns the bridge to
the Isle of Venus. In the richness of its ornament, it is remi-
niscent of one of those descriptions of ancient Rome which
Spenser, following Du Bellay, loved to give:[34]

It was a bridge ybuilt in goodly wize,
With curious corbes and pendants graven faire,
And arched all with porches, did arize
On stately pillours, fram'd after the Doricke guize.

(4.10.6)

As Scudamore passes over the bridge on foot, he notes:

The goodly workes, and stones of rich assay,
Cast into sundry shapes by wondrous skill,
That like on earth no where I recken may:

And underneath, the river rolling still
With murmure soft, that seem'd to serve the workmans
will.
(4.10.15)

Like an ancient river god who has been tamed by a bridge, a natural force has been brought into harmony with man's civilizing purpose as manifest in art, but this is only possible when neither art nor nature is abused; that is, when man's native sensuality is contained within the decorum of "seemly form."

If, then, one asks why evil art is so consistently shown as visual art in Spenser's poetry, the answer must lie in the sensual nature of the medium, and in its perils for unredeemed man. Although he does not attempt in so many words to explain why sensuality should be implicit in the Fall of Man, he shows through his story how the senses dangerously sway reason in the direction of their gratification. He demands that the visual arts be responsible; both their subject matter and their purpose must be judged by values outside themselves. Imitation, after all, is never just imitation; there is always some message conveyed by even the most naturalistic art, and it is this that compels assessment.

IV

But sensuous as the visual arts are in their appeal, their expressive powers are at the same time limited by this very appeal. Just as they cannot bestow immortal fame on any man because they themselves are tied to mortality, so their power to represent the invisible truth is restricted by their visible presence. To make this clear, Spenser resorts again to the *paragone,* suggesting that art can only hold a metaphorical relation to truth and that poetry understands this better than any other art.

Yet in alluding to the limits of the painter's or sculptor's
skill, he also points to the inadequacy of his own art in depicting the perfection of his queen:

> But living art may not least part expresse,
> Nor life-resembling pencill it can paynt,
> All were it Zeuxis or Praxiteles:
> His daedale hand would faile, and greatly faynt,
> And her perfections with his error taynt:
> Ne poets witt, that passeth painter farre
> In picturing the parts of beauty daynt,
> So hard a workemanship adventure darre,
> For fear through want of words her excellence to marre.
>   (3.Proem.2)

Since the direct portrait is impossible to achieve—"sith
that choicest witt / Cannot your glorious pourtraict figure
playne"—he will ask her pardon that he "in colourd showes
may shadow itt," as the cult of Isis shadowed justice in Book
V. He thus makes it clear that he is choosing metaphorical
expression over imitation as the only possible solution to the
problem of portraying absolute virtue. The "daedale hand"
suggests how far imitative art can go but also how limited it is
in expressing the spirit.

Just as no adequate portrait of the queen can be made, so
Spenser's beloved is beyond the scope of "daedale hand":

> The glorious pourtraict of that angels face,
> Made to amaze weake mens confused skill,
> And this worlds worthlesse glory to embase,
> What pen, what pencill, can expresse her fill?
> For though he colours could devize at will,
> And eke his learned hand at pleasure guide,
> Least, trembling, it his workmanship should spill,
> Yet many wondrous things there are beside.
> The sweet eye-glaunces, that like arrowes glide,

The charming smiles, that rob sence from the hart,
The lovely plesance, and the lofty pride,
Cannot expressed be by any art.
A greater craftesmans hand thereto doth neede,
That can expresse the life of things indeed.

(Am. 17)

The quest for the perfect portrait seems a futile one, yet even in describing its unattainability, Spenser is conveying something of what he says cannot be described. He of course rings the usual changes of the love sonnets on the subject of the lady's portrait, including the boast that it lies "most lively lyke in his heart" (45), but his use of the inexpressibility topos has a consistency throughout his works.[35] It is his conviction that true beauty is not "An outward shew of things that onely seeme" (*HB.*91),

Or why doe not faire pictures like powre shew,
In which oftimes we Nature see of Art
Exceld, in perfect limming every part?

(HB.82–84)

His quest for the perfect portrait is in fact made in full recognition that there can be no such thing. The *paragone* simply helps to show the impossibility of expressing the absolute, by alluding to the limitations of first one art, then another, until only the art of God is left to reveal, although it does not contain, the essence of beauty.

One of the topoi associated with the *paragone,* the fame of Apelles as the greatest painter of the ancient world, is particularly useful to Spenser. It matters little that he gives to him a story associated with another great artist of the ancient world—Zeuxis. Whether Zeuxis himself ever assembled five maidens of Crotona and took the best features from each in order to depict Helen of Troy, as Cicero relates, is equally unimportant. The story is concerned, not so much with the practice of a particular painter, as with the artistic problem of depicting absolute beauty.[36] Raphael in his famous letter to Castiglione also speaks of having to see many beautiful maidens in order to paint his Galatea. Spenser in his turn reminds us that the artist in pursuit of the ideal cannot find models here below:

> The Chian peincter, when he was requirde
> To pourtraict Venus in her perfect hew,
> To make his worke more absolute, desird
> Of all the fairest maides to have the vew.
>
> (*Ded.Son.* 17)

So he, Spenser, drawing "the semblant trew" of Queen Elizabeth, had to see many beautiful ladies of the court.

The same allusion serves just as well in Spenser's attempt to describe the beauty of Sapience in the *Hymne of Heavenly Beautie.* The difference in the passages is mainly one of context: in the commendatory sonnet, beauty is personified by the queen (with a lesser compliment paid to the beauty of the ladies of the court), while the beauty of Sapience calls for the emphasis to be placed even more forcibly on inexpressibility:

> Ne could that painter (had he lived yet)
> Which pictured Venus with so curious quill
> That all posteritie admyred it,
> Have purtrayd this, for all his maistring skill;
> Ne she her selfe, had she remained still,
> And were as faire as fabling wits do fayne,
> Could once come neare this Beauty soverayne.
>
> (ll. 211–17)

Yet the two passages are parallel in setting Spenser's task above Apelles's. The similarity is underlined, too, by Raleigh's commendatory sonnet, which says that the queen's virtue "can not be exprest, but by an angel's quill." Spenser's own comments on art, however, indicate not only a repetition of conventional topoi, especially the *paragone* along with other allusions to the well-known stories of ancient art, but also his real concern with the absolutes of love and beauty which no art can ultimately capture.

We are left with metaphor, a likeness, as the only means of representing the unrepresentable. As Plato and his followers, including Spenser, put it, man understands things only by an image, a likeness; he cannot know things in themselves but only analogically, by reflection. This is why *ut pictura* is so important as suggesting the poet's power of expression and why Sidney made it central to his definition of poetry. When poetry becomes picture, the medium itself turns metaphorical, like embroideries or inlaid woods that imitate painting. Thus freed from the limitations of his medium, the poet may create a new kind of likeness, one which will show the truth "with more light and better note."

All metaphors, as Spenser intimates time and again, are finally inadequate, but the good ones have divine guidance. His own great metaphor is his story, a mirror or picture of the soul caught in the web of sensuous experience. For him, the *paragone* of the arts with one another and with nature sums up the struggle to find and express the truth which lies beyond even the art of God, nature herself: "His seate is Truth, to which the faithful trust" (*HHB.*159).

NOTES

1. Plato, *Phaedrus,* 250. Cf. M. H. Abrams, *The Mirror and the Lamp* (Oxford, 1953), on the mirror as an image for mimesis.

2. See ch. 1, n. 6.

3. Puttenham, *Arte,* p. 19.

4. On the history of *ut pictura poesis,* see Rensselaer W. Lee, *Ut Pictura Poesis: The Humanistic Theory of Painting, Art*

Bulletin, 22 (1940), 197–269; rpt. New York, 1967. See also my article, "Media and Metaphors: Interpreting a Renaissance Analogy," *Acts of the Twenty-Second International Congress of the History of Art* (Budapest, 1972), 535–46.

5. Leonardo da Vinci, *Treatise on Painting,* trans. and ed. Philip MacMahon (Princeton, 1956), 1:161.

6. Ben Jonson, *The Forrest,* 13.43–44.

7. Sir Philip Sidney, *An Apology for Poetry,* ed. Geoffrey Shepherd (1965; rpt. Manchester, 1973), p. 102.

8. On the wall painting in *Lucrece,* see my article, "Mocking the Mind: The Role of Art in Shakespeare's *Rape of Lucrece,*" *Sixteenth-Century Journal,* 14 (1983), 13–22.

9. Leonardo da Vinci, *Paragone,* trans. Irma A. Richter (Oxford, 1949), p. 58: "adonque queste due poesie, o vuoi dire due pitture, hanno scambiati li sensi, per li quali esse dovrebbono penetrare all' intelletto."

10. Sidney, *Apology for Poetry,* pp. 101, 124.

11. Coignet, *Politique Discourses,* trans. Sir Edward Hoby (1586), selection in G. Gregory Smith, *Elizabethan Critical Essays* (Oxford, 1904), 1:342.

12. L. B. Alberti, *On Painting,* trans. John R. Spencer, rev. ed. (New Haven, 1966), p. 82.

13. Sabbia di Castiglione, "On the Decoration of the House," in R. Klein and H. Zerner, *Italian Art, 1500–1600: Sources and Documents* (Englewood Cliffs, N.J., 1966), pp. 23–24.

14. Lodovico Dolce, *Aretin: A Dialogue on Painting,* trans. W. Brown (1770), p. 77. Cf. Mark W. Roskill, *Dolce's "Aretino" and Venetian Art Theory of the Cinquecento* (New York, 1968), p. 121.

15. Puttenham, *Arte,* pp. 306–7.

16. See Jacopo Mazzoni, "On the Defense of the Comedy," selections in Gilbert, *Literary Criticism,* p. 363.

17. Vasari's place in the ekphrastic tradition is explained in Svetlana L. Alpers, *"Ekphrasis* and Aesthetic Attitudes in Vasari's *Lives," JWCI,* 23 (1960), 190–215.

18. Vasari, Preface to *The Lives of the Artists* (a selection), trans. George Bull (Harmondsworth, Eng., 1965), p. 27.

19. On the rivalry of the painter with nature, see the epitaph which Bembo composed for Raphael in Vasari, *Lives of the Artists,* p. 323:

> Ille hic est Raphael timuit quo sospite vinci
> Rerum magna parens et moriente mori.

> This is that Raphael, by whom in life
> Our mighty mother Nature fear'd defeat;
> And in whose death did fear herself to die.

20. See John Shearman, *Mannerism* (Harmondsworth, Eng., 1967), p. 21, for a discussion of *difficultà* as a hallmark of mannerist art. Incidentally, I cannot agree with Shearman's inclusion of Spenser within the ranks of so-called mannerist writers (p. 39). If John Lyly exemplifies a certain affectedness of style, the same cannot be said of Spenser. If one is in search of a stylistic label for him, then "High Renaissance" would seem more appropriate.

21. Ariosto, *Orlando Furioso,* trans. John Harington (1591), "An advertisement to the Reader," p. A^r.

22. John Hoskins, *Directions for Speech and Style* (1599), ed. Hoyt H. Hudson (Princeton, 1935), p. 8.

23. See J. A. Mazzeo, "St. Augustine's Rhetoric of Silence," in his *Renaissance and Seventeenth-Century Studies* (New York, 1964), p. 26, where he refers to the hierarchy of the arts, based on "the grade of rationality they contain, so that painting and sculpture rank well below music or literature." See also Edgar Wind, "Botticelli's Primavera," in his *Pagan Mysteries in the Renaissance* (New York, 1958), p. 127: "Concerning Ficino it is important to remember that, as a philosopher, he systematically placed the visual medium below the verbal."

24. Needless to say, this is not the gracious Cupid invoked at the beginning of the poem (Proem.1.3) or alluded to in the description of the angel's wings at 2.8.6; nor is he the re-

66 *The Spider and the Bee*

deemed Cupid of the Garden of Adonis (3.6.49). The Cupid of the House of Busirane has his destructive bow and arrows and is the object of shameful idolatry, like the Cupid of Sidney's *Astrophel and Stella* (5.5–8). In another context, however, Spenser puts himself in the company of worshippers of this same courtly-love Cupid. See *Muiopotmos*, ll. 97–104.

25. Only a Blatant Beast would break into "the sacred church." "And th' images, for all their goodly hew, / Did cast to ground, whilest none was them to rew" (6.12.25). Unless Spenser denied utterly his own sense of the beauty and value of art, he could never have sided with the indiscriminate rage of fanatical image-smashers. See his *View* 163 as cited in A. C. Hamilton's note on this passage in his edition of *The Faerie Queene* (London and New York, 1977).

26. Tasso is referring to a statement by Athanasius. See *Discourses on the Heroic Poem*, p. 36.

27. Cf. Pliny's story in *Natural History,* VII.127, and Lucian's in his *Icones,* 4; both writers associate it with the Cnidian Aphrodite of Praxiteles.

28. For a fuller discussion of this point, see my article, "*Muiopotmos:* A World of Art," *Yearbook of English Studies,* 5 (1975), 30–38. Spenser's selection of only one scene—Europa and the bull—from Arachne's tapestry suggests his awareness that this is the most pictorial of Ovid's series (*Metamorphoses.* VI.103–7), as well as the one that Ovid chose to represent most fully in his direct narrative, in II.843–75. Spenser's predilection for symmetry may also have played a part. By choosing only one scene, he can balance the single scene of Minerva's tapestry with a single one from Arachne's.

29. See Donne's Sermon XXIII.

30. E. H. Gombrich discusses this aspect of illusion in his *Art and Illusion,* 2d ed. (New York, 1961).

31. There is an ambiguity in the referent for the phrase "That seem'd and yet was not," but I do not agree with Isabel MacCaffrey (*Spenser's Allegory: The Anatomy of Imagination*

[Princeton, 1976], p. 117) that the referent is "mortall worke." It is not only mortal work that "seems," but divine as well. Her distinction between mortal "illusion" and divine "fiction" is, at best, dubious. I take the referent to be "it" — that is, the silveriness of the river. Cf. the passage in *An Hymne in Honour of Beautie,* mentioned on p. 61, where Spenser joins the beauty of art and the beauty of nature in order to deny that either of them possesses the essence of true beauty, which is spiritual: "Beautie is not, as fond men misdeeme, / An outward shew of things that onely seeme" (ll. 90–91). In other words, the beauty of the river is as illusory as the beauty of a work of art, except that it does not cater to avaricious tastes. Cf. my discussion of Spenser's deliberate ambiguity in his descriptions of illusionistic effects, pp. 184–86.

32. In E. K.'s gloss to the March eclogue of *The Shepheardes Calender,* Flora, the goddess of flowers, is referred to as "a famous harlot." Spenser possibly has this aspect of the goddess in mind in the Bower of Bliss passage; at least Flora has been transformed from virgin to harlot by the ministrations of Art.

33. On the friendship of art and nature, see A. Kent Hieatt, *Chaucer, Spenser, Milton* (Montreal, 1975), pp. 102–13.

34. Cf. *Ruines of Rome.* xxix. On the relationship of the bridge to the river, I am again indebted to A. Kent Hieatt, *Chaucer, Spenser, Milton,* p. 105.

35. On "inexpressibility topoi," see E. R. Curtius, *European Literature and the Latin Middle Ages,* trans. W. R. Trask (New York, 1953), pp. 159–62.

36. On the artist's pursuit of absolute beauty, see Erwin Panofsky, *Idea,* trans. Joseph J. A. Peake (Columbia, S.C., 1968). With Spenser's own quest for beauty, compare Sidney's reference to David the Psalmist as "a passionate lover of that unspeakable and everlasting beauty to be seen by the eyes of the mind, only cleared by faith" (*Apology for Poetry,* p. 99).

CHAPTER 3

The Rhetoric of Illusion

If *ut pictura poesis* seemed to Renaissance critics to sum up
the poet's mimetic mode of art in general, it also had a
particular relevance to narrative poetry, where the unfolding
of an action must be presented chiefly through description
rather than through dialogue, as on the stage. When Spenser
stated that his purpose in writing his allegory was to conceal
good discipline under "an historicall fiction" and when he
compared himself to "the antique poets historicall," as well as
to contemporary epic poets, he showed his willingness to be
bound by the principles of narrative poetry, whose task is to
provide "feigned history" as it might be recorded by an
eyewitness.[1]

The eyewitness account given by the poet is in fact at
the center of Sidney's advocacy of the didactic value of poetry which combines "the general notion with the particular
example":

> For, as in outward things, to a man that had never seen
> an elephant or a rhinoceros, who should tell him most
> exquisitely all their shapes, colour, bigness, and particu-
> lar marks, or of a gorgeous palace, the architecture, with
> declaring the full beauties might well make the hearer

68

able to repeat, as it were by rote, all he had heard, yet should never satisfy his inward conceits with being witness to itself of a true lively knowledge: but the same man, as soon as he might see those beasts well painted, or the house well in model, should straightways grow, without need of any description, to a judicial comprehending of them.[2]

It may seem paradoxical that Sidney should dismiss "description" in an account of what poetry can do better than philosophy, when description is the poet's very medium. Clearly, he is dramatizing the poet's ability to transcend the medium of words and make the reader see—the ability of poetry to "satisfy" the "inward conceits" of the reader "with being witness to itself of a true lively knowledge." The key words— "witness" and "lively"—appear in one form or another in virtually all allusions to description. A seemingly casual reference in Shakespeare's *Henry V* dwells upon the paradox of a "lively" evocation of the Battle of Agincourt, where so many thousands are dying:

> Description cannot suit itself in words
> To demonstrate the life of such a battle
> In life so liveless as it shows itself.
> (IV.ii.53–55)

The inexpressibility topos once again—yes, but here it contains a reminder that the ordinary function of description is to bring to life.

In the rhetorical tradition of *ekphrasis,* already mentioned as gaining special prestige in the elaborate description of works of art, the emphasis is always on "bringing before one's eyes what is to be shown." Schoolboy practice in these set descriptions of "persons, actions, times, places, seasons, and many other things" no doubt affected the patterning of Spenser's descriptions, reminding him of the need to "bring about seeing" through hearing, by including a sufficient number of details and by placing the object in relationship to other things. This rhetorical device also encouraged him to think of description as not only visual in its effect but decorative in its form, a set piece to arouse the admiration of the listener. Although such a view of description may seem to run counter to narrative movement, Spenser had enough of the romance sense of story to carry him onward, while at the same time he was able to turn the decorative aspects of *ekphrasis* to advantage for his symbolic purpose. This decorative aspect of his imagery will be examined more fully in the following chapter; first, however, some attention must be given to his actual method of attaining illusion.

The demand that a story make us see is both an ancient one and a modern one, and so the relationship of *ekphrasis* to narrative need not be belabored. Hermogenes notes that "some precisians do not make ecphrasis a (separate) exercise on the ground that it has been anticipated both in fable and in tale . . . for in these too they say we expatiate descriptively on places, rivers, deeds, and persons."[3] If we turn to the words of someone nearer our own time, we find exactly the same association of fiction and eyewitness account. To Henry James, the "air of reality (solidity of specification)" seemed the supreme virtue of the novel: "It is here in very truth that he [the novelist] competes with life; it is here that he competes with his brother the painter in his attempt to render the look of things, the look that conveys their meaning, to catch the colour, the relief, the expression, the surface, the substance of the human spectacle."[4]

Among Elizabethan critics there is no doubt that narrative requires the painter's art, or what Puttenham calls "hypotiposis or the counterfait representation": "The matter and occasion leadeth vs many times to describe and set foorth many things, in such sort as it should appeare they were truly before our eyes though they were not present, which to do it requireth cunning."[5] Even more cunning, as everyone knew, was required to depict things purely imaginary—"not naturall or not veritable"—for here the poet-painter may have no examples to follow. But the immediate criterion for images both natural and phantastic was credibility. When Peacham wishes to define "efficacie," he says that it consists in "presenting to our minds the liuely *Idaea's* or formes of things so truly, as if wee saw them with our eyes; as the *places in Hell*, the fiery Arrow of *Acesta*, the description of *Fame*, the flame about the Temples of *Ascanius*,"[6] and so on.

Spenser too is unashamedly a painter when he writes as a storyteller. The argument prefixed to "Februarie" in *The Shepheardes Calender* fitly sums up the relation between narrative and pictorial vividness: "the olde man telleth a tale of the Oake and the Bryer, so lively and so feelingly, as, if the thing were set forth in some picture before our eyes, more plainly could not appeare." In varying terms, similar praise has been lavished almost universally upon *The Faerie Queene* ever since it first was published.[7]

Yet to discuss Spenser's images in the stylistic terms used for paintings—as, for example, his handling of perspective and space—is to make of *ut pictura poesis* something much more literal than I believe the Renaissance meant by the phrase.[8] It was not a stylistic analogy at all but one based upon the expressive powers of the image—what it says to the human heart. Like all analogies, the limits of the comparison are as important to observe as its validity, and the fundamental difference in media should make us cautious of seeking to explain the poet's images through their supposed use of pictorial methods.

Perhaps we need a psychology of inner perception, a study of how language expresses and stimulates the image-producing faculty of the mind.[9] But it may be that our best information will have to come from those who, like Edmund Burke, are masters of introspection. Not satisfied that words can, or ought to, produce the equivalent of a painting in the mind, he noted that words "affect us in a manner very different from that in which we are affected by natural objects, or by painting and architecture"; and, anticipating Lessing, he went on to conclude that the business of poetry and rhetoric is "to affect rather by sympathy than imitation; to display rather the effect of things on the mind of the speaker or of others, than to present a clear idea of the things themselves."[10] More tellingly, Giraldi Cinthio in his 1554 treatise *On Romances* discusses *enargeia* or vivid description in terms that go beyond psychological effect and touch the very essence of poetic creation:

> It also seems to me that the words can be so significant and so apt in revealing the thoughts as to be impressed on the reader's mind with such efficacy and vehemence that one feels their force and is moved to participate in the emotions under the veil of words in the poet's verses. This is the *Enargeia,* which does not reside in the minute . . . but in putting the thing clearly and effectively before the reader's eyes and in the hearer's ears, assuming that this is done artfully with appropriate words (to which the ancients gave dignity for their own quality) which are, as it were, born together with the thing.[11]

There could be no better justification for our turning to the rhetorical tradition, rather than to the psychology of visual perception, in order to understand the kind of illusion which Spenser provides for readers of *The Faerie Queene.*

It may seem paradoxical that the sympathetic response of which Burke speaks should be evoked by the highly formalized descriptive schemes that Spenser uses. In literature, as in painting, we tend to think of stylization as substituting pattern for illusion. For Spenser's attainment of illusion, we must therefore ultimately look to the way the descriptive schemes become part of the speaking voice of the poet-narrator. Meanwhile, it may be noted that these schemes do indeed lend themselves to the evoking of fantasy images since they allude to familiar concepts in the clearest way possible, aiming at consistency of effect but with sufficient gaps in the information to enlist the reader's imagination. For any kind of person, place, thing, or occasion, the traits, originally derived from the places of invention, are predetermined. As Faral notes, a very complete doctrine, more than we can discover from the *arts poétiques,* must have existed on the subject of description.[12] Certainly formulas lay to hand for describing scenes of council, battles, women on horseback, mixed forests, wild forests, earthly paradises, rich palaces— to mention only a few of those clichés which originated in the topoi or places of invention.[13] We are concerned here, however, not with the history of particular topoi but with the kinds of schemes or formal patterns by which rhetoric gave official recognition to the role of description in the adornment of style.

The simplest and most direct of the descriptive schemes that Spenser used were those concerned with the description of person, place, and action. These, of course, are so essential to the progress of the narrative that they have as their chief office the presenting of a clear picture. They do not go beyond the straightforward enumeration of the attributes of things; these are the figures "which do chiefly respect circumstances and adiuncts without form of comparison seruing onely to make matters euident and lightsome."[14] In seeking to present a picture these schemes must employ literal language, emphasizing the objective characteristics of whatever they describe. This is exactly Spenser's method in, for example, the description of the gentle knight:

> A gentle knight was pricking on the plaine,
> Ycladd in mightie armes and silver shielde,
> Wherein old dints of deepe woundes did remaine,
> The cruell markes of many' a bloody fielde;
> Yet armes till that time did he never wield:
> His angry steede did chide his foming bitt,
> As much disdayning to the curbe to yield:
> Full jolly knight he seemd, and faire did sitt,
> As one for knightly giusts and fierce encounters fitt.
>
> (I.I.I)

The formulaic character of the language is particularly evident in the noun/adjective combinations, such as "gentle knight," "mightie armes," "deepe woundes," "angry steede," "foming bitt." These adjectives, with their familiar mode of emphasis, act as allusions to the tradition of chivalric romance, but they are no longer otiose in being used primarily to meet some metrical requirement; now they are carefully selected with a view to making a definitive image.[15] With this goal ever in mind, Spenser develops his descriptions more fully than is usual in the metrical romances and fits them to his stanza as to a frame which will set them off as picture. The more outward appearance of the knight is portrayed in one stanza; his inward life and purpose are adumbrated in the following stanza, with the help of the symbolic cross on his breastplate and on his shield; but attention continues to be directed to his appearance, including his facial expression, which "did seeme too solemne sad." The way the word "seem" echoes through the first two stanzas of the poem already presents the central issue of the poem: the interpretation of appearances.

It is of the essence of the descriptive schemes that they purport to give an objective portrayal of something. Even the qualitative effect is treated as if it were objective, and not as if it had reference to the sensibility of the poet. The evaluative implications of the adjectives ("gentle" or "cruell," for example), far from designating the poet's subjective response, merely indicate the acceptance of fixed standards and their usefulness in assigning a meaning to objects.[16] Thus description in Spenser aims above all at identification. In fairyland what we require is just such identification, if we are not to lose our bearings.

Is it not clear then why Spenser's instrument of description is the adjective and not the metaphor?[17] As Shakespeare uses metaphor, an aura of suggestion is brought to the enhancement of reality; but Spenser deliberately limits suggestion for the sake of focusing attention on the reality of the objects he has in view. If he does use a metaphor, it is either a very commonplace one, limited in its powers of suggestion by the frequency of its use; or it is used purposely to introduce some extraneous note, something beyond the mere appearance, such as sarcasm or irony:

> But foolish mayd! whyles, heedlesse of the hooke,
> She thus oft times was beating off and on,
> Through slipperie footing fell into the brooke,
> And there was caught to her confusion.
>
> (5.5.43)

So he writes of the deceitful Clarinda, the Amazon's maid, who was caught in her own trap. But in the ordinary course of description Spenser has no need of metaphor for what he wants to convey, which is simply the three-dimensional reality of things. He is creating a whole world to act as a metaphor; he is too busy in that task to do more than tell us what this world looks like.

We shall better understand the solidity of Spenser's world if we observe his following of the descriptive schemes, with their methodical assembling of attributes.[18] The description of a person, called *prosopographia,* was defined as "a forme of speech by which as well the very person of a man as of a fained, is by his form, stature, maners, studies, doings, affections, and such other circumstances seruing to the purpose so described, that it may appeare a plaine and liuely picture painted in tables, and set before the eies of the hearer." Any of the portraits from Spenser's gallery will do to illustrate the sort of circumstances which might be chosen to present a person. The palmer who accompanies Guyon is depicted by means of details concerning his appearance and character:

> Him als accompanyd upon the way
> A comely palmer, clad in black attyre,
> Of rypest yeares, and heares all hoarie gray,
> That with a staffe his feeble steps did stire,
> Least his long way his aged limbes should tire:
> And if by lookes one may the mind aread,
> He seemd to be a sage and sober syre,
> And ever with slow pace the knight did lead,
> Who taught his trampling steed with equall steps to tread.[19]
>
> (2.1.7)

This is a "plaine picture" because it includes a sufficient number of sensuous particulars such as the color of the palmer's garb and of his hair, the staff needed to support his feeble steps, his restraining effect upon his companion's steed. But the suprasensuous function of the portrait is also evident. *Prosopographia* was not only intended to present a picture but "to praise, to dispraise, to delight, to engraue in perpetuall memory the description of great persons." Here we find a cautious, but not the less weighty, praise for "a sage and sober syre." Every picture contains a judgment for which the details provide the evidence.

A ready narrative justification for Spenser's frequent use of *prosopographia* lies in the unexpected encounters that are so typical a feature of fairyland. Sir Calidore, near the beginning of Book VI, having vanquished Crudor,

> is on his former way,
> To follow his first quest, when as he spyde
> A tall young man from thence not farre away,
> Fighting on foot, as well he him descryde,
> Against an armed knight, that did on horsebacke ryde.
>
> (6.2.3)

A general description follows, first of a lady "standing on foot, in foule array," then of the sudden killing of the armed knight. When Calidore draws near enough to observe the appearance of the young man in detail, we are given a two-stanza description:

> Him stedfastly he markt, and saw to bee
> A goodly youth of amiable grace,
> Yet but a slender slip, that scarse did see
> Yet seventeene years, but tall and faire of face,
> That sure he deem'd him borne of noble race.
> All in a woodmans jacket he was clad
> Of Lincolne greene, belayd with silver lace;
> And on his head an hood with aglets sprad,
> And by his side his hunters horne he hanging had.
>
> Buskins he wore of costliest cordwayne,
> Pinckt upon gold, and paled part per part,
> As then the guize was for each gentle swayne;
> In his right hand he held a trembling dart,
> Whose fellow he before had sent apart;
> And in his left he held a sharpe bore-speare,
> With which he wont to launch the salvage hart
> Of many a lyon and of many a beare,
> That first unto his hand in chase did happen neare.
>
> (6.2.5–6)

Only three lines, the first two and the fifth, contain reminders that we are being shown the youth, Sir Tristram, as Calidore views him, and these lines deliver a judgment of character. The rest of the details are so decorative in effect that they are

like a painting or tapestry. In such a set piece, as the poet
moves from the age of the youth to his heredity to his dress
and to his occupation—all standard topics in the description
of a person—it seems that Spenser is being influenced by the
classical tradition of *ekphrasis.* Perhaps he knew the *Imagines*
of Philostratus. Certainly, the separableness of these elaborate descriptions and the richness of detail suggest that he
thought of description as a work of art which vies with the
painter's.

Descriptions of places, known as *topographia,* as Spenser
uses them are designed chiefly to reflect the character of the
persons who dwell in them. This purpose is not directly indicated in such definitions of this scheme as Peacham gives: "an
euident and true description of a place . . . countries, cities,
townes, temples, pallaces, castles, walles, gates, mountains,
vallies, fields, orchards, gardens, fountaines, dens, and all
other maner of places." But when Sherry says, "now may you
see what Amplification riseth by the circumstances belonging
to persons & thynges,"[20] we find a clue to Spenser's habit of
making setting an extension of the person, in order that the
character of the person may be brought out more emphatically. So, for example, the description of Belphoebe's paradise reflects the serenity of her being:

> Into that forest farre they thence him led,
> Where was their dwelling, in a pleasant glade
> With mountaines rownd about environed,
> And mightie woodes, which did the valley shade,
> And like a stately theatre it made,
> Spreading it selfe into a spatious plaine;
> And in the midst a little river plaide
> Emongst the pumy stones, which seemd to plaine
> With gentle murmure that his cours they did restraine.
>
> Beside the same a dainty place there lay,
> Planted with mirtle trees and laurells greene,

In which the birds song many a lovely lay
Of Gods high praise, and of their loves sweet teene,
As it an earthly paradize had beene:
In whose enclosed shadow there was pight
A faire pavilion, scarcely to be seene,
The which was al within most richly dight,
That greatest princes living it mote well delight.

(3.5.39–40)

This is another set piece, a typical *locus amoenus,* but as a
scene in nature it is appropriately more simple and less decorative than the portrait of Tristram, with his rich attire. The
first stanza creates a secluded scene, set apart from the disorder of the world; the second stanza suggests the dwelling of a
love goddess and hints at the paradox of Belphoebe's nature,
aloof and chaste, yet seductive in her way, as Timias is all too
aware of. Essentially, Spenser's *topographiae* express a sympathetic relation between man and his surroundings, a sense
that he involuntarily seeks out a place in keeping with his
state of mind. As Britomart wanders to the raging sea in her
distress, so Timias in his melancholy finds a solitary
abode:

And finding there fit solitary place
For wofull wight, chose out a gloomy glade,
Where hardly eye mote see bright heavens face,
For mossy trees, which covered all with shade
And sad melancholy: there he his cabin made.

(4.7.38)

The sensuous details transparently express an idea: the mossy
trees cover everything not only with shade but with melancholy.

Imaginary places were sometimes treated under a separate
rhetorical category known as *topothesia,* of which the main
purpose was to suggest a mystery rather than to describe a

definite place. But in Spenser's poetry, the distinction does
not seem altogether relevant, since everything is imaginary
anyway. Perhaps Peacham's definition of *topothesia* applies
particularly to Spenser's caves: "a fained description of a
place, that is, when the Orator describeth a place, and yet no
such place: As is the house of enuy in the 6 booke of
Metamorphosis, the house of sleepe in the eleuenth booke, or
else when the place is not such a one as is fained to be, as in
heauen and hell. In the fourth booke of *Aeneidos.*" Descriptions of this sort were appropriately more vague and shadowy
than descriptions of actual places; Tasso in his directions for
describing things specified that the poet "should not show
feigned things in the light of the sun, but rather in darkness,
like goods that in that way are more easily sold."[21] One thinks
of the House of Morpheus in Book I or the Cave of Mammon in Book II, with its "faint shadow of uncertein light; /
Such as a lamp, whose life does fade away; / Or as the moone,
cloathed with clowdy night, / Does shew to him that walkes
in feare and sad affright" (2.7.29). Another dark place is the
house of the Fatal Sisters:

> Farre under ground from tract of living went,
> Downe in the bottome of the deepe Abysse,
> Where Demogorgon, in dull darknesse pent,
> Farre from the view of gods and heavens blis,
> The hideous Chaos keepes, their dreadfull dwelling is.
>   (4.2.47)

The more remote from human experience the place is, the
more Spenser preserves the mystery by not giving specific
details but largely relying on the evocativeness of his words.

A figure using more detail is *pragmatographia,* which presents a picture of an action, or, as Peacham calls it, "a
description of things," by "gathering together all the circumstances belonging to them . . . as if they were most liuely

painted out in colors & set forth to be seene. . . . To this
figure belong the descriptions of warres, tempestes, ship-
wrackes, conquestes, tryumphes, destructions of citties and
countries, murders, open shewes, dearths and deathes." This
figure, too, may be used "to amplifie" as well as "to declare
things plainly" and "to moue pittie." All three purposes are
implied in the battle scenes of *The Faerie Queene.* Since in
describing an action the poet is just as concerned to be pictorial as he is in describing a person or place, he must treat it as
a series of scenes, each complete in itself. A particularly
lovely "description of things" recounts the journey that Marinell's mother took to rescue him in his wounded state:

> Great Neptune stoode amazed at their sight,
> Whiles on his broad rownd backe they softly slid,
> And eke him selfe mournd at their mournfull plight,
> Yet wist not what their wailing ment, yet did,
> For great compassion of their sorrow, bid
> His mighty waters to them buxome bee:
> Eftesoones the roaring billowes still abid,
> And all the griesly monsters of the see
> Stood gaping at their gate, and wondred them to see.
>
> A teme of dolphins, raunged in aray,
> Drew the smooth charett of sad Cymoent;
> They were all taught by Triton to obay
> To the long raynes at her commaundement:
> As swifte as swallowes on the waves they went,
> That their brode flaggy finnes no fome did reare,
> Ne bubling rowndell they behinde them sent;
> The rest of other fishes drawen weare,
> Which with their finny oars the swelling sea did sheare.
>
> Soone as they bene arriv'd upon the brim
> Of the Rich Strond, their charets they forlore,
> And let their temed fishes softly swim
> Along the margent of the fomy shore,

Least they their finnes should bruze, and surbate sore
Their tender feete upon the stony grownd:
And comming to the place, where all in gore
And cruddy blood enwallowed they fownd
The lucklesse Marinell, lying in deadly swownd.

(3.4.32−34)

Each stanza marks one phase of the action, turning it into a
self-contained scene, with first a glimpse of Neptune's realm
and his power; next, the smooth, swift journey of the dolphins as they draw Cymoent's chariot; and last, the arrival
on the shore where Marinell lies wounded. Moreover, the
theme of compassion is sounded three times: first by Neptune, who stills the waters out of sympathy for the nymphs'
sorrow; then by the nymphs themselves as they protect the
tender feet of the dolphins by letting them swim "along the
margent of the fomy shore"; and finally by the description of
Marinell "enwallowed" in his "cruddy blood" and "lying in
deadly swownd." The following stanza describes how Cymoent herself swoons with grief and her nymphs join their la-
ment to hers. All of the "circumstances," such as the watching
sea monsters and the team of dolphins, help to amplify the
mother's emotion while at the same time suggesting a world
apart, where the "watry sisters" play and grieve with equal
abandon. Even when sorrow touches them, it is somehow
remote from us and rather like Venus and Adonis in the
tapestry description of Book III, where the goddess, for all
her grief, transforms the dead Adonis to "a dainty flower." As
Spenser suggests, we cannot expect the grief of the immortals
to disfigure them; their world is not ours, and we can only
look on them with wonder.

This example shows how the poet can take a time-bound
sequence and transform it into pictures, which themselves
imply a before and after but depict a present, much as great
narrative painting always does. The painter, of course, has to

choose the "pregnant moment" but it is the greatness of a Titian, in his *Rape of Europa* or *Venus and Adonis,* to be able to make us see the before and after in the particular dramatic moment he has chosen to depict. When Spenser turns action into picture he has the liberty provided by his medium to show each moment of a drama, in an unfolding sequence, but in thus turning action into picture, he attains the *enargeia* that is the goal of all narrative art.

The other descriptive schemes which Spenser uses are less narrative in intent and more patently rhetorical; they use language not so much to make us see a picture as to underline the significance or the momentousness of an event. *Cronographia,* the description of time or season, usually contains a periphrasis "for delectations sake." But the circumstances accompanying the use of this figure may very properly serve to amplify an occasion. Such a description as the following lends weight to a great enterprise; it supplies a sense of the dedication and excitement preceding heroic action:

> The morrow next appear'd, with purple hayre
> Yet dropping fresh out of the Indian fount,
> And bringing light into the heavens fayre,
> When he was readie to his steede to mount,
> Unto his way, which now was all his care and count.
>
> (5.10.16)

Beyond the narrative importance of telling the time of day, *cronographia* plays a part in the emotional context for any action, and that is why Spenser likes to begin and end episodes with this figure.

A figure that is less common in *The Faerie Queene* is *icon.* Peacham says that since "this forme of speech is a singular iewell of eloquence, so ought the vse thereof to be very rare." It is a cumulative scheme, a piling up of similes in order to present a picture of a person or thing; we must so read it as to grasp the sum or total effect of all these similes. That is what Peacham means by his definition of *icon* as "a forme of speech which painteth out the image of a person or thing, by comparing forme with forme, qualitie with qualitie, and one likenesse with another." For example, Spenser uses an *icon* to depict the horror of the dragon's eyes:

> His blazing eyes, like two bright shining shieldes,
> Did burne with wrath, and sparkled living fyre;
> As two broad beacons, sett in open fieldes,
> Send forth their flames far of to every shyre,
> And warning give, that enimies conspyre
> With fire and sword the region to invade;
> So flam'd his eyne with rage and rancorous yre:
> But far within, as in a hollow glade,
> Those glaring lampes were sett, that made a dreadfull
>   shade.   (1.11.14)

The details in this figure do not have separate allegorical significance, but they induce a single emphatic emotional response. Moreover, the patterned effect of the *icon* contributes to its impact; the repetition of simile upon simile within the limits of the stanza scheme gives the figure a peculiarly concentrated force. Spenser uses it only for extremes: for the uncovering of Duessa, to show total ugliness; for the flight of Florimell, to show the extremity of fear. This figure, for all its sensuous details, tends to leave picture behind in its intention of underlining a concept.

Finally, the "counterfait representation" may take the form of *prosopopoeia*, which may be a personifying of inanimate objects, very like what a later century called the pathetic fallacy; or which may be a granting of speech to animals, as in *Mother Hubberds Tale*. This figure is defined as "the faining of a person, that is, when to a thing sencelesse or dumbe we faine a fit person," and has for its uses, "to complaine, to accuse, to reprehend, to confirme, and to commend." The rhetorical function of this figure is manifestly to enhance the emotion of an occasion: when the gods assembled on Arlo Hill, Mole the mountain decked himself in his freshest attire in honor of Dame Nature. To make more vivid ("to confirme and make his [the poet's] cause euident") the allegorical significance of the wedding of the rivers, they are personified with all their train:

> Therefore on either side she was sustained
> Of two smal grooms, which by their names were hight
> The Churne and Charwell, two small streams, which
>   pained
> Them selves her footing to direct aright,
> Which fayled oft through faint and feeble plight:
> But Thame was stronger, and of better stay;
> Yet seem'd full aged by his outward sight,
> With head all hoary, and his beard all gray,
> Deawed with silver drops, that trickled downe alway.
>   (4.11.25)

The pictorial detail inspired by the use of this figure is entirely figurative, since it is a projection of the poet's idea through imagined activities in the world of nature.

At last we come to what many readers assume to be the most pictorial parts of the poem, or what they think of when imagery is mentioned—the epic simile. Undoubtedly this figure uses sensuous detail to build a picture, such as the image of a shepherd brushing away gnats on a summer evening, or of a falcon flying at a flush of ducks, or of a housewife in her dairy. But these images have no narrative burden to carry, being indeed set off from the narrative by "like" or "as"; their purpose, therefore, is purely to illustrate concepts:

> Like as in sommers day, when raging heat
> Doth burne the earth, and boyled rivers drie,
> That all brute beasts, forst to refraine fro meat,
> Doe hunt for shade, where shrowded they may lie,

> And missing it, faine from themselves to flie;
> All travellers tormented are with paine:
> A watery cloud doth overcast the skie,
> And poureth forth a sudden shoure of raine,
> That all the wretched world recomforteth againe.
>
> (4.4.47)

This image illustrates sudden comfort brought to the oppressed; whether or not it is "a simile from observation" is irrelevant.[22] It was not for realism that the Elizabethans commended similes, but for their usefulness in giving "profit by their perspicuitie, and pleasure by their proportion." In Spenser they may enhance the narrative by enriching and confirming our understanding of a battle, a state of mind, a wonderful scene.

As for the figure *allegoria* itself, Spenser uses it occasionally as a kind of allegory within the whole allegory of the poem.[23] When he does, the effect is unmistakably nonsensuous; unlike the descriptive schemes we have been considering, *allegoria* does not paint a picture by using literal language. Instead, it is a metaphor, which we instantly translate because we are so directed. When Britomart in her lovesickness comes to the seacoast and sits down on the rocky shore, there is a brief picture of the scene before her: "Tho, having vewed a while the surges hore, / That gainst the craggy clifts did loudly rore" (3.4.7). But when she compares her troubled state of mind to the raging sea, it is not our eyes but our minds that are engaged by the pointed and very familiar symbolism:

> "Huge sea of sorrow and tempestuous griefe,
> Wherein my feeble barke is tossed long,
> Far from the hoped haven of reliefe,
> Why doe thy cruel billowes beat so strong,
> And thy moyst mountaynes each on others throng,
> Threatning to swallow up my fearefull lyfe?

O! doe thy cruell wrath and spightfull wrong
At length allay, and stint thy stormy stryfe,
Which in these troubled bowels raignes and rageth ryfe."
(3.4.8)

This is not narrative allegory but meditative or emblematic allegory. It does not tell a story but interprets the significance of the scene for the character who views it. Britomart's interpretation, including her references to Love as her "lewd pilot" and Fortune as her "boteswaine" that "no assurance knowes," keeps the reader's attention on the parallel between her emotional situation and the physical scene before her. Despite the conventional quality of this allegory—it is widespread in Petrarchan love poetry and in emblem books—Spenser is able to put new life into the cliché by his narrative context: the plight of Britomart and the actual sea setting.

Yet *allegoria* remains entirely different from the descriptive schemes with their task of creating a picture and advancing a narrative. That is not to say that the whole of *The Faerie Queene* is not an allegory, but only that in Spenser's larger allegory he is telling a story, which requires that he create images of persons, places, and actions as they exist in themselves and not simply as comparisons for something else. On the other hand, his inset *allegoriae* do have this relatively simple end: to use concrete things for point-by-point comparison with an abstraction. Such images we must translate because they have no existence apart from their meaning, whereas the literal imagery of the narrative—here Britomart's actual seashore—creates a world of its own to act as a larger kind of metaphor. It is in the making of this larger metaphor that the art of the allegorist comes close to the art of the novelist by painting a picture of life itself.

When Sidney claimed for the poet the ability to present an image without "description," he was thinking of the moving power of the poetic image, a power which Leonardo claimed for painting alone. It is the poet's pictures, says Sidney, which give a "more familiar insight" into the nature of man: "all virtues, vices, and passions so in their own natural seats laid to the view, that we seem not to hear of them, but clearly to see through them."[24] If Spenser's descriptions are to work according to Sidney's didactic theory, they too must leave words behind and create an illusion which transcends the additive and linear sequence of words, to suggest a whole that can be taken in at a glance. And here we should not underestimate the power of his story to transform even the most detachable ekphrastic description into illusion.[25] His constant stress on the factual reality of what he describes is supported by his allusive style, giving the impression that the image does indeed exist independently of the narrator, who has only to draw our attention to its salient features. In so doing, the poet speaks to "the eye of mind," engaging our imaginations to complete the illusion.

From the art of the bee to the art of the spider—that is the true mystery of Spenser's imagery. We have seen him using rhetorical patterning to make each image self-contained and complete, almost as though it were an ornate definition of a concept. But these descriptive schemes only appear to define; it is of their nature, rather, to supply a frame, to delimit an area within which the reader's imagination is set free, on the same principle as the one that governs the relationship between expressive form and restrictive form in the poem as a whole. Just as the allegory controls the larger units, so the descriptive schemes are latticelike forms for marshaling details[26] which in themselves need be no more allegorical than those that occur in the account of Tristram's attire but that make their contribution to the larger scheme of things. Not using details for point-by-point comparison with abstractions, Spenser opens the way to all the richness of his narrative illusion. In the words of Coleridge: "Observe also the exceeding vividness of Spenser's descriptions. They are not, in the true sense of the word, picturesque [or picturelike], but are composed of a wondrous series of images, as in our dreams."[27]

The descriptive schemes, as Spenser uses them, in all their conventionality of detail, tacitly recognize that language can do no more than remind us of what we already know or have imagined. The eighteenth-century philosopher Dugald Stewart commented on the beholder's share: "In Poetry, and in every other species of composition, in which one person attempts, by means of language, to present to the mind of another, the objects of his own imagination; this power is necessary, though not in the same degree, to the author and to the reader. When we peruse a description, we naturally feel a disposition to form, in our own minds, a distinct picture of what is described; and in proportion to the attention and interest which the subject excites, the picture becomes steady and determinate."[28] But it must be added that Spenser's art is no mere triggering of free-floating imagery: we return to his words, because they are beautiful in their selection and ordering and because they fashion a work of art which exists only in that particular form. When he uses the descriptive schemes and fits them to his stanza, with its segregating alexandrine, he shapes his images ornamentally. To that aspect of his art, the significance of ornament, the next chapter is devoted.

NOTES

1. On epic as history and on the necessity of changing even history itself into fable in an epic, see Cinthio, *On Romances,* pp. 19, 167.
2. Sidney, *Apology for Poetry,* p. 107.

3. Cited in C. S. Baldwin, *Medieval Rhetoric and Poetic* (New York, 1928), p. 36.

4. Henry James, "The Art of Fiction," *The House of Fiction,* ed. Leon Edel (London, 1957), p. 33.

5. Puttenham, *Arte,* p. 238.

6. Henry Peacham, *The Compleat Gentleman* (1634) (Oxford, 1906), p. 84.

7. For some modern reactions against the old view of Spenser as the painter among poets, see: Rudolph Gottfried, "The Pictorial Element in Spenser's Poetry," *ELH,* 19 (1952), 203–13; Lyle Glazier, "The Nature of Spenser's Imagery," *MLQ,* 16 (1955), 300–310; C. R. Sonn, "Spenser's Imagery," *ELH,* 26 (1959), 165–70. More influential than these, however, is Paul Alpers, *The Poetry of The Faerie Queene* (Princeton, 1967).

8. See my article "Style and the Mind's Eye," *JAAC,* 38 (1979), 325–34.

9. For recent research on mental imagery, see, for example, *The Function and Nature of Imagery,* ed. Peter W. Sheehan (New York, 1972); Frank S. Kessel, "Imagery, a Dimension of Mind Rediscovered," *British Journal of Psychology,* 63 (1972), 149–62; and two articles in *NLH,* 7 (1976): Michael Rio, "Images and Words," 505–12, and Gillian Cohen, "Visual Imagery in Thought," 512–23. On the pictorial in Spenser as imitating the processes of perception, see John B. Bender, *Spenser and Literary Pictorialism* (Princeton, 1972). See also my review of Bender's book in *JEGP,* 72 (1973), 550–52.

10. Edmund Burke, *A Philosophical Enquiry into the Origins of the Sublime and Beautiful* (1757), ed. J. T. Boulton (London, 1958), pp. 163, 172.

11. Cinthio, *On Romances,* p. 135.

12. Edmond Faral, *Les Arts Poétiques du XIIe et du XIIIe Siècle* (Paris, 1924), p. 83.

13. See Curtius, *European Literature and the Latin Middle Ages.*

14. Henry Peacham, *The Garden of Eloquence* (1593), p. 135.

15. Cf. Susan Wittig, *Stylistic and Narrative Structures in the Middle English Romances* (Austin, 1978), ch. 1.

16. See Josephine Miles, *Major Adjectives in English Poetry from Wyatt to Auden* (Berkeley, 1946), p. 362, for a comment on the adjectives in this passage.

17. The simile may also appear in a modest way, since the "like" or "as" so clearly signals its function that it does not jeopardize the literalness of the description.

18. I take the definitions for the rhetorical figures from Peacham's *Garden of Eloquence* (1593), pp. 134–46. For a survey of Spenser's use of rhetoric, see H. D. Rix, *Rhetoric in Spenser's Poetry* (University Park, Pa., 1940). But Rix has not considered in any detail the relation of particular figures to the various genres.

19. One of the differences between description in Spenser and Ariosto is that generally Spenser brings in more circumstances and thereby provides a fuller picture than Ariosto. With Spenser's portrait of the palmer, compare *Orlando Furioso,* trans. W. S. Rose (London, 1864), II.12 and 13:

> a hermit in a valley
> Devotion in his aspect was expressed,
> And his long beard descended on his breast.
>
> Wasted he was as much by fasts as age,
> And on an ass was mounted, slow and sure;
> His visage warranted that never sage
> Had conscience more precise or passing pure.

20. R. Sherry, *A Treatise of the Figures of Grammer and Rhetorike* (2d ed., 1555), sig. Gii[r].

21. Tasso, *Discourses on the Heroic Poem,* in Gilbert, *Literary Criticism,* p. 490. See also Cavalchini and Samuels's trans. of the *Discourses,* p. 52.

22. The phrase comes from A. A. Jack, *Chaucer and Spenser* (Glasgow, 1920), p. 349.

23. *Allegoria* is regularly defined as a long or continued metaphor, and is, therefore, considered a trope and not a scheme.

24. Sidney, *Apology for Poetry,* p. 108.

25. Cf. Suzanne Langer, *Feeling and Form* (New York, 1953): "A course of impersonal happenings is a strong framework for the making of a poetic illusion; it tends to become the ground plan or 'plot' of the entire piece, affecting and dominating every other means of literary creation" (p. 261).

26. See Curtius, *European Literature and the Latin Middle Ages,* on "the lattice of form," p. 390.

27. *Coleridge's Miscellaneous Criticism,* ed. T. M. Raysor (Cambridge, Mass., 1936), p. 35.

28. Cited in Wolfgang Iser, *The Implied Reader* (Baltimore, 1974), p. 79.

CHAPTER 4

Image as Ornament

If structure supplies both order and purpose, it is ornament which supplies beauty. Spenser fashions his images decoratively, as well as illusionistically, in a continuum which is determined by the degree of action occurring at any given moment. The more action, the less ornament, according to the principle that whenever narrative interest quickens, illusion will take precedence over pattern. This yielding of decorative intent is, in a sense, natural; for example, when the narrative dominates, there can be no time to pause for such an elaborate description as the one of Belphoebe (2.3.21 – 31). But no violation of Spenser's art occurs when he is being either simply illusionistic or decoratively intricate. Where untruth sometimes enters is the moment when the didactic steps forth with none of the winsomeness that Sidney finds essential to the teaching of virtue. But in general, Spenser has intuitively followed Sidney's dictum, as well as explicitly endorsed it in his prefatory letter: "seeing all things accounted by their showes, and nothing esteemed of, that is not delightfull and pleasing to commune sence." The deprecatory tone should not deceive us: behind the apparent concession to the reading public lies the artist with all the commitment to beauty implied in Colin Clout's vision of the Graces dancing. A sermon in plain terms was not his style. What was his style was a magical world of beauty realized in decorative form.

It is as well to note, too, that in spite of the importance attached to artistic illusion during the Renaissance, it was not to be achieved at the cost of an ornate style. We may think of this style as produced not only by using words arranged according to rhetorical patterns but also by treating description as a form requiring a subject matter with intrinsic artistic interest. Holding to the view he expressed in the *Hymne of Beautie,* "That wondrous paterne . . . Is perfect Beautie," Spenser consciously attempts to reproduce that beauty on earth through his art. If his pursuit of illusion results in a dreamlike sequence of images for the reader, his pursuit of ornamental beauty results in a tapestrylike effect. But like illusionistic paintings of the late medieval and early Renaissance period, no conflict need be felt between these two aspects: the words can seem to "lose their verbality" in the fictional world they create, or they can seem to form a decorative pattern by the way they are chosen and arranged for beauty. The descriptive schemes discussed in Chapter 3 are designed to accomplish both.

The opposition between illusion and ornament is thus not absolute but complementary. After all, ornament is frequently illusionistic (the ivory waves on the gate of the Bower of Bliss), and illusion is frequently ornamental (the ornamental patterns attached to Florimell's streaming hair). The battle scenes mentioned in Chapter 1 were themselves designed to be both narrative illusion and decorative showpieces. This in-and-out effect, whereby we can either be absorbed in the narrative illusion or be conscious of the pattern of description, may even be considered essential to the poem as allegory. If we remained caught by the illusion, as in reading a novel, we might well miss some of the allegorical significance. It is the transformation of the purely visual into the decorative that helps to turn the transitory world of phenomena into an enduring object of contemplation; and, as we shall see, the world seen as art also provides a basis for the examination of the purposes of art.

Aesthetic considerations here have none of the usual implications of art for art's sake, because the ordering of the parts, as of the whole, is from the Renaissance point of view the adornment of truth. In the words of Thomas Nashe, "true things are rather admirde if they be included in some wittie fiction, like to Pearles that delight more if they be deeper sette in golde."[1] The jewelry metaphor aptly conveys Spenser's whole approach to his task and may help to explain why the structure of the small units—namely, the stanzas—is so much more finely articulated than the structure of the larger canto units or the books themselves.[2] Thinking as he does mainly in terms of the perfection of the parts, he remains to some extent unaware of a need to subordinate them to a larger unity. Nevertheless, the poem as a whole, like the cosmos, is intended to have both order and ornament. It is only because lapidary ornament captures more of the artistic imagination of someone like Spenser that it becomes almost the whole of art and the meeting point of considerations both moral and aesthetic.

But he, the poet of the beautiful, has traveled some distance from the attitude he expressed in *Muiopotmos*.[3] There, the aesthetic point of view prevailed: a universe of exquisite order left little room for tragedy, or indeed for heroic action. Butterflies and spiders were equally part of this tapestrylike universe of art. It is true that the life-affirming values were represented by the butterfly and the death-dealing by the spider, that moral distinctions were drawn, and that the butterfly was identified with the good, the spider with the evil. Nevertheless, within the confines of the genre—mock-heroic epyllion—the morality of art was something that Spenser could not fully confront. Clearly, too, it is only in a world of butterflies and spiders that the aesthetic attitude could dominate so completely over emotion and tragedy. With epic, on the other hand, the realm of human action is entered. Art cannot be all, once the universe is viewed as an arena for heroic struggle. Whereas the butterfly could not struggle, his accoutrements being merely decorative, the heroes of *The Faerie Queene* wear real armor. No longer is the good embodied in a helpless butterfly, doomed from the start, but in a Britomart, triumphant with her sword. In this context, where moral fiber is tested, art itself must come under scrutiny.

In *Muiopotmos,* it will be recalled, art was essentially divine art—either the work of gods or of nature, which is the art of God. But art, originally identified with the divine, may become the work of the devil, a notion already implied in the intricate beauty of the spider's web. But whereas the spider worked within the bounds of nature, the mind of evil man brings to both art and nature the possibility of sin. Those who use art for evil purposes pervert it, much as those who, like Hellenore, follow "beastly lust" pervert nature.

Aesthetic success can, then, no longer be the sole criterion of value. It is not enough that art should exhibit a perfect skill, such as the tapestries of Castle Joyous and the House of Busirane do; they may still be admired as art but must be condemned in purpose because they are traps far more deadly than the spider's web, strangling the soul and not just the body. In other words, although evil may still be seen to play its part in the economy of the universe, it is now to be resisted and, if possible, defeated, even in its most seductive guise. In place of the detachment of *Muiopotmos,* there is an engagement between narrator and reader, as there is between the emotions of the narrator and those of the characters who concern him. And so the tapestry of life turns into a battlefield while, paradoxically, retaining its decorative surface.

But how are we to come to terms with a mode of perception that selects the ornamental features in nature, in people, in architecture, in battles, in dragons—in short, in everything—while at the same time asking us to take seriously the moral struggle between equally patterned elements? Of course, this kind of perception is enshrined in common Elizabethan usage, in everything from embroidery to architecture, as well as in such poetry as Marlowe's and Drayton's. But Spenser's is a particularly acute eye for the decorative line, which he can find even in the personification of evil, the dragon of Red Cross's mortal combat:

His huge long tayle, wownd up in hundred foldes,
Does overspred his long bras-scaly back,
Whose wreathed boughtes when ever he unfoldes,
And thicke entangled knots adown does slack,
Bespotted as with shieldes of red and blacke,
It sweepeth all the land behind him farre,
And of three furlongs does but litle lacke;
And at the point two stinges in fixed arre,
Both deadly sharpe, that sharpest steele exceeden farr.
                                    (1.11.11)

Such a heraldic beast must necessarily be modeled on literary and artistic examples; his very distance from nature invites decorative treatment.

Yet nature itself to Elizabethan writers generally was scarcely less a subject for verbal embroidery, as the following example from Abraham Fraunce's *Third Part of the Countess of Pembroke's Yvychurch* shows:

Fresh-colored medowes were ouer-spread with a mantle
Figured, and Diapred with such and so many thousand

> Natures surpassing conceipts, that maruelus *Iris*
> Was no maruel at al, and spotted traine, but a trifle,
> Prowd-hart Peacocks spotted traine, compar'd to the
>   matchles
> Art, which nature shewd, in shewing so-many strange
>   shewes.[4]

Nature, wild and untamed in her negative aspects, is in her positive as artistic as she knows how to be; this is the final cause which directs her efforts:

> For all that Nature by her mother wit
> Could frame in earth, and forme of substance base,
> Was there, and all that Nature did omit,
> Art, playing second Natures part, supplyed it.
>
> (4.10.21)

Sometimes she achieves perfection; often she cannot because the substance is resistant, or because her "mother-wit" is inadequate. As things strive toward what Spenser saw as the masculine, immortal perfection of art, this is as God intended, and in harmony with nature at her best. Where art pursues earthly female goals, such as Acrasia's spiderlike propensities dictate, it supports nature in her negative aspect only.[5] But it is a single perception which holds together everything in *The Faerie Queene,* good and evil alike, and that perception is essentially focused on the decorative detail.

As artist, the writer takes his cue from God, the divine craftsman. What God bestowed upon his creation was beauty; what man should give in response is wonder: "Who is not astonished to behold the rich garments of the beasts of the field, and the birds of the ayre, rich in their proud mantles, their glorious maynes, their beautiful backes, their soft feathers, their comely spottes, their glittering wings? Who wondreth not at the hair of the Lyon, the spotted garment of the Panter . . . who can sufficiently display the beauty of the

Cock, the rich tale of the Peacocke, the innumerable colours of the Pigeon, the glorious feathers of the Fesant?"[6]

This is the model set before the earthly craftsman, and it is a model in which the decorative features are the significant ones. God was not content with mere function to express his joy in creation, or so it seemed to the Renaissance writer, who knew nothing of evolution and the survival value of the colors and markings of earthly creatures.[7] Just as we tend to find in function the sole justification for what we see, so the Renaissance tended to find in nature the very ornamental qualities that we might consider superfluous, if not actually the antithesis of the natural: "There were hills which garnished their proud heights with stately trees, humble valleis, whose base estate seemed comforted with refreshing of silver rivers: meadows enameled with al sorts of eye-pleasing flowres: thickets, which being lined with most pleasant shade, were witnessed so to by the chereful disposition of many wel-tuned birds."[8] As this passage from *The Arcadia* indicates, even if Sidney calls nature brazen as compared with the golden nature of the poets, he is thinking of art as an intensification of qualities already present in nature, not as a denial of these qualities. The earth may never have given forth such sweet-smelling flowers as the poets describe but it does indeed give forth flowers and thereby serves as a model for the poets. Not for nothing are the poet's figures of speech called "flowers of rhetoric," for they imitate the divine example by adorning the plain prose of ordinary discourse as flowers may adorn the plain prose of a common field.

In fact, the *deus artifex* is a more significant idea than at first appears. It is not simply the divine skill of earthly craftsmen that is represented in this notion, marvellous though the metal work of an Achilles' shield may be. Rather, to see God as the supreme artificer, whether in metal, paint, or tapestry, as the Renaissance did, is to find the universe fundamentally based on aesthetic values: when God created man, He fashioned him as a sculptor who works in clay would; the whole of nature is a splendid painting.[9] Perhaps we can find a clue in Ficino's expression "the ornament of forms," which he used to describe the imposition of order upon chaos.[10] This relationship between ornament and orderliness can be seen, for example, in Spenser's description of the garden at the Temple of Venus:

> walkes and alleyes dight
> With divers trees, enrang'd in even rankes.
>   (4.10.25)

If form itself is essentially ornament, then ornaments are the most intricate and refined of forms. In the subject matter of Spenser's descriptions one can see all the gradations from waste wilderness, which is closer to chaos, to the ultimate works of art and nature, where one is virtually indistinguishable from the other. It is this decorative conception of form that makes the theory of ornament comprise almost the whole of Renaissance aesthetic.[11]

Certainly, no Renaissance artist could rest content with the bare bones of logic or function to constitute a work of art. It was beauty alone that could be called the final expression both of God and man ("Beauty," according to Buoni, is "the looking glasse" of God.),[12] and to beautify one's work meant to add ornament. What is extraneous becomes paradoxically essential. In rhetoric, an architectural metaphor was often used to describe the relationship between a logical statement and the embellishments which transform it into a work of art. Fracastoro turns this architectural metaphor into a regular defense of ornament:

> if columns and peristyles and other things are added to
> houses, they will be extraneous, for the barest structure
> will serve the purpose of a house, which is to protect us

from storm and cold. But indeed if he consider objects as they should be, and look for perfection, these additions will not only not be extraneous but essential. Or ought we to think splendid garments extraneous because poor ones are sufficient? Do you not see that just as perfection and ornament are a real part of the things which nature produces, so they are of the things which art produces? What perfection and beauty are, only the great artists know. And if you take them away from the subject, assuredly you have somehow taken away life itself. Therefore what the painters and the poets add to things for perfection is not extraneous, if we mean by "thing" not the bare object such as common artificers, or those who are controlled and restricted by some purpose make, but the object perfected and given life.[13]

Again, it is to be noted that nature has set the example for the use of ornament. Wherever perfection, rather than the requirements of utility, is the goal, then ornament is there to supply luster, as well as significance. For Quintilian, ornament means going beyond the merely lucid;[14] for Alberti, it is something added—"an auxiliary Brightness and Improvement"—to the beauty of proportion.[15]

Yet such terms as "Brightness" and "perfection" suggest too little to us to bring home the meaning of ornament. Perhaps "significance" comes closer to identifying its value in language we can understand. For example, when Artegall's helmet, sword, and shield are stripped from him by the Amazon Radigund, they are described as "the ornaments of knightly name." At this moment, the symbolic value of these objects transcends their usefulness; it is as significance, as depth revealed upon the surface, that ornament was considered essential to the expressiveness of a building, an object, a person, truth itself. Ungarnished, how can anything reveal its meaning? An allegorical narrative, from this point of view, might be considered an adornment of truth, a fine play of wit that delights in pattern and intricate workmanship. For, as Equicola puts it, "The invention, without ornament, is a mass of gold that does not shine."[16]

To understand Sidney's golden world, then, we have to try to recapture the state of mind in which ornament stood as a symbol of the nobler, brighter, happier. Today, an aesthetic puritanism has decreed that ornament is, at best, trivial; at worst, dishonest. The word "functional," as I have already indicated, alone seems to guarantee authenticity, even in Rosemond Tuve's valiant defense of Renaissance poetic. It is true that the machine age has made ornament largely obsolete, simply because machine-made ornament is a contradiction in terms. The most essential element of ornament—its preciousness—is missing, for where everything is standardized, nothing can be precious.

But in courtly art, the precious is the visible sign of prestige and position, symbolic both of the divine and of the princely. If one looks at a Renaissance portrait such as Baldovinetti's *Lady in Yellow*, the loving care given to the pattern on the lady's sleeve shows just this taste for the ornamental.[17] But foliage, the natural world itself, takes on these decorative qualities in Botticelli or Nicholas Hilliard. Similarly, the intertwining of the voices in a madrigal embroiders the text. Even language was to be viewed as a medium that lent itself to decorative effect. Puttenham can talk of figurative speech as like the "passements of gold" that beautify a princely garment;[18] no one can praise a plain or unadorned style. Rhetoric had become identified with elocution, much as architecture had become identified with decoration.

An epic poem such as *The Faerie Queene* belongs to a genre which has the specific purpose of praise and which therefore requires all the courtly ornaments:

> But, O dredd Soverayne,
> Thus far forth pardon, sith that choicest witt
> Cannot your glorious pourtraict figure playne,
> That I in colourd showes may shadow itt,
> And antique praises unto present persons fitt.
>
> (3.Proem.3)

These ornaments of epic poetry could be seen as everything from the unhistorical order to the meter, fiction, and episodes—everything, that is, that may decorate and illuminate.[19]

For the adornment of truth and the creation of a golden world, the poet has two methods at his disposal—things and words. First, he may give his subject a golden flavor by allusions to precious objects, such as gold and jewels, in his descriptions and comparisons. The very mention of pearls, gold, and precious gems was enough to give pleasure since the naming of these objects was, for the Renaissance, to conjure up an image of them. Naming and image-making became identical. This method of giving precious things "a virtual presence" in the poetry would then be equivalent to the use of gold and ultramarine in painting of the early quattrocento. But the poet could also make his style golden by embellishing it with figures of speech, elegant diction, and rhetorical devices of all kinds.[20] As complementary aspects having the same purpose, both methods set a high value on poetry as distinct from the prose of everyday life. Ornaments have thus not only social and religious prestige, but stylistic; the same hierarchy of values prevails and places elocution, gold, and jewels, at the very top of the scale.

In a sense, ornament is only possible in relationship to structures, whether of society or of artistic creation. It is the reward of obeying the law of restrictive form, of "beeing contained within the walles of a roome," as Peacham says of soft music.[21] Though ornament is a freedom into which the artist escapes, it is a licensed freedom within delimited space, such as the margins of a manuscript or the confines of the epic simile. Principles of decorum leave the artist less free to express himself according to his own whim than free to make patterns pleasing to the eye or ear. Although tradition might supply the basic patterns, their elements could be reshaped into new combinations or their whole effect changed by translation into a new medium as, for example, a translation of an emblem from a book into a piece of embroidery. In every field, the Renaissance was truly "an era of decorative invention."[22] Significantly, the definition of "play" is virtually identical with the definition of "ornament." Absolved from the needs of function, "play marks itself off from the course of the natural process. It is something added thereto and spread out over it, like a flowering, an ornament, a garment."[23] Beyond the clarity and correctness of neoclassical criteria, the Renaissance subscribes to a value to be conveyed only by the superfluous gesture, the flourish. But if, as Fracastoro puts it, "what is added makes manifest the perfection and excellence of the subject, ought we not to concede for all its great usefulness and desirability?"[24]

The adjective, as Spenser uses it, may be considered as one of those superfluous gestures.[25] Why should grass be identified as "green" or skin as "alabaster"? According to Erasmus, this is a usage permitted in poetry rather than in prose, presumably because these epithets are purely ornamental. But they are also forms of praise, intensifying the best connotations of the noun being modified.[26] Of all words of praise, none is higher than "golden," so Spenser gives us "the golden quill of the poet" or "Apollo's golden brood."

To make more impressive, he may extend the adjective "golden" into a simile, as in the following description of Britomart's hair:

And round about the same, her yellow heare,
Having through stirring loosd their wonted band,
Like to a golden border did appeare,
Framed in goldsmithes forge with cunning hand:
Yet goldsmithes cunning could not understand
To frame such subtile wire, so shinie cleare.
For it did glister like the golden sand,
The which Pactolus, with his waters shere,
Throwes forth upon the rivage round about him nere.
                                                                    (4.6.20)

Nature, the art of God, has here surpassed the art of man, for no goldsmith would have the art to frame "such subtile wire, so shinie cleare." In place of the goldsmith's wire, Spenser puts the golden sands of the River Pactolus as a more lavish image, drawn from nature but rich in mythological connotations. The unbounded desire of Midas met its natural boundary in the remorseless logic of his wish; yet he left a beauty behind in the river he touched, which became literally what Shakespeare's "gilding pale streams with heavenly alchemy" was metaphorically. Spenser's is this realm of the mythical, of the larger than life; and although the mythical is a mode of the metaphorical, it is couched in literal terms; hence the materialism or sensuous appeal through which the highest values are presented.

This is one basic source of misunderstanding of Spenser's use of ornament: what was once part of the more real is now part of the less real, for we have no metaphysics of light which would make bright, jewel-like things closer to the divine than dark, heavy things. The kind of justification that the Abbot Suger used for his accumulation of treasures for St. Denis is simply not available to us. Not for us, therefore, the effect of the loveliness of jewels which take Suger away from external cares to "some strange region of the universe which neither exists entirely in the slime of the earth nor entirely in the purity of heaven."[27] Nor for us the values of a Ficino which make all material lights a reflection of the Father of Lights. It is the secularization of ornament in the modern world, no less than the domination of the machine over the work of men's hands, that has made ornament obsolete.

The cost of the precious materials adds to their metaphorical and mythical value a dimension that is important. As Gombrich says, Suger would not have been brought to a religious trance by tinsel.[28] Gold has other values than its glitter: not only is it indestructible, but its acquisition requires a certain sacrifice of time, effort, and other things, and so it becomes fit for royalty: "Royally clad . . . in cloth of gold." It is set apart from ordinary life, as Puttenham and Peacham say that the language of poetry should be. Precious objects are uniformly contrasted with the meaner properties of brass, iron, lead, or clay: "Nor shining gold, nor mouldring clay it was." As a metaphorical image, gold is, then, a shorthand expression for the highest value seen in all its luminosity, not as a harsh doctrine. The too much loved earth becomes more lovely; virtue is not to be avoided as a threat to pleasure. Instead, the golden wings of love and the golden trumpet of epic will inspire both our eyes and our thoughts.

All the diverse forms of ornamentation are linked by light-reflecting surfaces, such as those which adorn Sapience in the *Hymne of Heavenly Beautie:*

> And all with gemmes and jewels gorgeously
> Adornd, that brighter then the starres appeare,
> And make her native brightnes seem more cleare.
>   (ll. 187–89)

For this is the point: the ornaments are right when their metaphorical significance matches the quality of what they adorn. The heavens themselves are decorated with a thousand lamps of burning light and with ten thousand gems of shining gold, while Sapience wears on her head a crown of "purest gold," in sign of highest sovereignty.

At the same time, the decorative use of gold and jewels implies pattern and workmanship. Alma's train is "Braunched al with gold and perle most richly wrought"; Britomart's armor is "all fretted round with golde." The interest in decorative effect extends to hair that is "crisped like golden wyre" and, equally, to a squire's bugle that "hong adowne his side in twisted gold / And tassels gay" (1.8.3). Like the "curious trayles" and "the crisped hair," the "twisted gold" suggests that liveliness of surface interest which the eye can follow with most delight. It is the craftsman's skill, even more than the precious materials, which never fails to arouse the narrator's enthusiasm. But this respect for the godlike power of the artist to recreate nature in a variety of media is widespread: both Suger and Dolce, for example, comment on how "the value of gold and even the richest gems is greatly enhanced if a cameo or intaglio, designed and executed by an ingenious artist, representing an elegant figure is enchased or engraved upon it."[29] In the history of art criticism, the painter's virtuosity was becoming far more valuable than the gold he used in his work.[30]

A specific aspect of craftsmanship is variety in pattern-making. This is not only commended in Spenser's descriptions, as are other aspects of decoration, but is also demonstrated in the descriptions themselves. This is a technique that poets need not confine themselves to praising but can also practise. But it makes sense only in relationship to an idea of order and regularity of structure; for, as Milton, speaking about variety in building, explains, from these "brotherly dissimilitudes that are not vastly disproportionall arises the goodly and gracefull symmetry that commends the whole pile and structure."[31] On the other hand, one cannot very well think of variety as an important principle in modern poetry, simply because irregularity of form and absence of fixed patterns often make variations irrelevant. Variety means something only when order determines form.

In Spenser's use of the descriptive schemes, we have one kind of amplification which also meets the demand for variety, but the main types of varying mentioned, for example, in Hoskins's *Directions for Speech and Style* are forms of repetition, ranging from alliteration to patterns that use the same word or words in different positions. In *The Faerie Queene,* Spenser has no hesitation in using alliteration quite freely:

> As beauties lovely baite, that doth procure
> Great warriours oft their rigour to represse,
> And mighty hands forget their manlinesse.
> (5.8.1)

He is sparing of the more elaborate kinds of repetition:

> No tree, whose braunches did not bravely spring;
> No braunch, whereon a fine bird did not sitt;
> No bird, but did her shrill notes sweetely sing;
> No song, but did containe a lovely ditt:
> Trees, braunches, birds, and songs were framed fitt
> For to allure fraile mind to carelesse ease.
> Carelesse the man soone woxe, and his weake witt
> Was overcome of thing that did him please;
> So pleased, did his wrathful purpose faire appease.
> (2.6.13)

Indeed, the very ornateness of the verbal patterning here helps to suggest "false delights" and "pleasures vain." Yet in another context, such as the catalogue sonnet "Ye tradefull merchants" (*Am.* 15), positive praise can similarly take the form of musical variations on a theme. This is not something to be apprehended on a strictly intellectual plane, in spite of Rosemond Tuve's insistence that "a greater intellectual richness" is "one of the most important implications of the demand for variety";[32] we have, rather, to see variety as that decorative fitness which nature achieves only by a lucky chance but which art more consistently pursues.

As the opposite of ornament is bareness, so the opposite of variety is monotony. Against these criteria, one may wonder how the classical values of restraint and unity can possibly count for much. Some of the critics say outright that variety pleases more than unity, as Malatesta does when defending romance against epic: "If we look closely at the nature of the soul, it is clear that it derives special pleasure from the variety of things and, on the contrary, special boredom and fatigue from their uniformity and identity."[33] If nature herself so delights in variety that she lavishly decks the fields with flowers, Aristotle's recommendation of unity could seem to run counter to her example. Thus Spenser refers to the garden of *Muiopotmos* as adorned "with all variety," while his prologue to Book VI of *The Faerie Queene* alludes to this "delightfull land of Faery" with its ways

> so exceeding spacious and wyde,
> And sprinckled with such sweet variety
> Of all that pleasant is to eare or eye,
> That I, nigh ravisht with rare thoughts delight,
> My tedious travell doe forget thereby.
> (6.Proem.1)

Yet though a meadow may be "paynted all with variable flowers," the "forms are variable and decay": delightful as Nature is in its variety, it is subject to decay through its changeableness. It seems that variety is a characteristic of the mutable realm, though, as the Mutability Cantos make clear, Nature's sergeant, Order, oversees the whole. In nature as in art, variety must be strictly contained in the kind of "rooms" defined for it. The *horror vacui* of Gothic meets the Renaissance insistence on harmony.

But there is a true carelessness of art that is beyond calculation. It is as though this carelessness is the point at which nature and art meet:

> And whether art it were, or heedelesse hap,
> As through the flouring forrest rash she fled,
> In her rude heares sweet flowres themselves did lap,
> And flourishing fresh leaves and blossomes did enwrap.
>
> (2.3.30)

The musical confusion of hounds and horns in *A Midsummer Night's Dream* is of this kind, where nature and art become virtually the same. Sidney's *Arcadia* illustrates a similar concept: "In the dressing of her haire and apparell, she might see neither a careful arte, nor an arte of carelesnesse, but euen left to a neglected chaunce, which yet coulde no more vnperfect her perfections, then a Die anie way cast, could loose his squarenesse." And again, "and so farre from all arte, that it was full of carelesnesse; vnlesse that carelesnesse it selfe (in spite of it selfe) grew artificiall."[34] This is the variety of disorder but still a kind of controlled confusion that enhances, does not detract from, beauty. It is like the use of language in *The Shepheardes Calender,* as E. K. sees it:

> But all as in most exquisite pictures they use to blaze and portraict not onely the daintie lineaments of beautye, but also rounde about it to shadow the rude thickets and craggy clifts, that, by the basenesse of such parts, more excellency may accrew to the principall (for oftimes we fynde our selves, I knowe not how, singularly delighted with the shew of such naturall rudenesse, and take great pleasure in that disorderly order) even so doe those rough and harsh termes enlumine and make more clearly to appeare the brightnesse of brave and glorious words. So oftentimes a dischorde in musick maketh a comely concordaunce: so great delight tooke the worthy poete Alceus to behold a blemish in the joynt of a wel shaped body.[35]

In other words, art that is too perfect may incur the charge of monotony. It will also be too remote from nature, some of whose own decorative features take the form of "trayles," the wandering line of nature.

In fact, irregularity or roughness is not simply an attempt to come closer to untamed nature; it provides its own decorative effect through the general principle of variety within order. It is part of the aesthetic success of the Bower of Bliss that it observes this principle: "So cunningly the rude / And scorned parts were mingled with the fine." These rude parts are like the crags and roughnesses that E. K. praises in style. And a concord is shown, in that art and nature beautify each other's work and "agreed through sweet diversity / This gardin to adorne with all varietie." Similarly, the base murmur of the water meets the silver-sounding instruments. Here, ironic praise must be read in the light of Renaissance aesthetic ideals, to which in many ways the Bower conforms.

It closely resembles, for example, a garden scene in the *Hypnerotomachia,* where Nature herself is an artist: "Betwixt the curious twistings of the braunches and their green leaues, the white flowers did aboundantly shewe themselves a singular Ornament, breathing foorth a most delectable and sweete odour. And to please the eye, the faire fruit was in no place wanting, where it should yeelde content."[36] But the writer's vision shows him, too, the work of a "cunning Artificer" who could reproduce nature in precious metals and stones to decorate a courtyard. He sees "either a vyne or some Woodbine of Golde . . . with diuers fashioned leaues of green emeralde . . . and the flowers dispersed and distributed of Saphires and byrrals. And with an excellent disposition and artificial, betwixt the green leaues and the grosse vaynes, so precious hunge down the clusters of grapes made of stones, agreeable and fitting to the natural coulers of Grapes."[37] All this is "curious workmanship" rather than deception.

Yet if the context is changed, exactly the same sort of art may become the object of the moralist's ire. When measured by a dream of pastoral innocence, golden ivy and grapes made of precious stones, not to mention the more lascivious aspects of the Bower, can seem like that courtesan type of eloquence which Sidney condemns: "Now for the outside of it [poetry], which is words, or (as I may term it) diction, it is even well worse. So is that honey-flowing matron eloquence apparelled, or rather disguised, in a courtesan-like painted affectation."[38] Although the ornamental style — "the fashioning of our language to delight" — is generally regarded as the persuasive style (and is so used in the Bower), rhetorical handbooks caution against the overuse of verbal ornaments. There must be "store, though not excess of terms."[39] Critics of both art and literature shared a distaste for overornamentation, which Quintilian described as a body that is all eyes.[40] Alberti, too, remarked that "the soul is delighted by all copiousness and variety," but he wanted neither an overcrowding nor a loss of dignity and truth; he will not permit the variety of figures and objects to turn into confusion.[41] It is significant that in the Garden of Adonis everything "is rankt in comely rew." For in the Garden, as well as in the Bower, moral allegory acts as a form of stylistic criticism. A world too golden becomes a critique of the golden style.

Falsity can of course overtake all symbols of value and give them the opposite significance. Gold becomes evil when it is in Mammon's store or carried by Avarice. Similarly, the luster is absent in Lucifera's false glory as she sits decked "in glistering gold and pereless pretious stone." An excess and an inappropriateness have robbed these symbols of their proper significance, turning them instead into a mere show, like false rhetoric with its golden words hiding a hollow meaning. In these descriptions of evil glitter, the metaphor *ironia* expresses a criticism that the words themselves do not

display. Spenser seems to be praising when he is in fact dis-
praising, using the same kind of description for both purposes. Even the word "pure" can become ironic: "Of purest
gold was spred a trayle of yvie"; and the true purity is seen to
lie in scorning gold as Britomart does on the Precious Strand:
"but would not stay / For gold, or perles / or pretious stones."

For Spenser, the whole problem of art is the problem of
ornament: how it is to be brought into right relationship with
the good. What we today may not grasp is the *mana* of ornament. If it cannot enchant us, as it enchanted Abbot Suger,
neither can it frighten us with its demonic power. In some
ways, the Puritans, including Savonarola, understood ornament better than we do, for, fearing its influence, they also
understood its power. Once dissociated from the divine, it no
longer enhances innate beauty but is a substitute. On the
other hand, true beauty, even without ornament, possesses
its own value, as can be seen, for example, in the description
of Britomart's face when Artegall has disarmed her at their
first encounter:

> With that, her angels face, unseene afore,
> Like to the ruddie morne appeard in sight,
> Deawed with silver drops, through sweating sore,
> But somewhat redder then beseem'd aright,
> Through toylesome heate and labour of her weary fight.
>
> (4.6.19)

Her only adornment is, as already noted, her golden hair.
Corruption of the meaning of ornaments inevitably leads to a
demand for simplicity—Una and Britomart—or a desire to
see virtue as a jewel plain set. But nature herself has a way of
using ornament to dress the good. The aged man called
Contemplation, whom Red Cross meets during his stay at the
House of Holiness, is simplicity itself and yet is adorned with
"snowy lockes,"

> As hoary frost with spangles doth attire
> The mossy braunches of an oke half ded.
>
> (1.10.48)

Although the good needs no adornment, it alone deserves it, and nothing can change the value-charged symbols of the precious, not even their misappropriation by the evil ones. The Heavenly City continues to dazzle the sight with its walls and towers built of "perle and precious stone," which are so far beyond the natural that "earthly tong / Cannot describe, nor wit of man can tell." Spenser's devout sense of what is fitting keeps him from turning into a Puritan iconoclast even as it keeps him from limiting his conception of decorum to merely decorative appropriateness.

The fact is that Spenser's genre, as he defines it, requires the ornamental style. But in choosing to describe everything in terms of art, so that his images are faceted like jewels, he is not only meeting Renaissance criteria of beauty; he is choosing, as well, to establish the sense of distance and stillness that will keep us from getting lost in the illusion and will allow us to contemplate the images as symbols. Their decorative quality is precisely related to their emblematic origins and emblematic functions. Just as Elizabethan decoration was itself "universally emblematic,"[42] so Spenser turns his emblems into ornate images. Consider, for example, his description of Prays-desire, the "faire fresh" but "sad and solemne" young lady, complete with poplar-branch attribute, whom Arthur meets at the Castle of Alma:

> In a long purple pall, whose skirt with gold
> Was fretted all about, she was arayd;
> And in her hand a poplar braunch did hold.
>
> (2.9.37)

The stylization of emblem, its already simplified forms, permits its transfer into new media, such as embroidery or plaster work, but, at the same time, a real artist like Spenser can bring a fresh vitality to his emblems by lending them the beauty and significance of his entire invention.

Even the relatively more three-dimensional figures of *The Faerie Queene,* such as Britomart or Una, are decoratively contained within the allegorical scheme. Nothing can break out of this almost geometrical framework. So compelling is it that Spenser virtually limits himself to devising variations on such themes as chastity or knightly valor by arranging and rearranging the words that by tradition will convey the concepts.

We have already noted the description of the dragon in the static brilliance of its heraldic form. But even Duessa in her unveiling or Error in her native ugliness become grotesque pieces of decoration, unlike Milton's Sin, the vastness of whose horror cannot be contained by ornamental definition. Stylization at once reduces the emotional impact of Spenser's images and appeals to the reader's sense of pattern. As there is more immediacy in Milton, more personal involvement, so there is more detachment, more of a friezelike effect in Spenser; as Milton is more dramatic, as well as more self-conscious, so Spenser adheres more closely to the highly wrought surface decoration of the goldsmith's art, in which richness, refinement, and polish count for more than the intensity of expression at which Milton aims.[43]

For Spenser, as for the Middle Ages and most of the Renaissance, description *is* decoration. He would not have understood Lessing's objection to the enumeration of parts such as Ariosto gave in his portrait of Alcina;[44] rather, he would have agreed with Dolce, who says that in this description Ariosto shows "how justly good poets may be deemed painters. This description I shall ever retain, as an invaluable jewel, in the treasure of my memory."[45] But if the long enumerative set piece is exceptional as a jewel, Spenser knows that it should be used sparingly. What distinguishes him from lesser poets of this era is his greater craftsmanship, so that he does not add more richness of jewels or gold out of a naive love for their glitter. He knows that selection and ordering of details can give an image decorative value, whether these details are in themselves rich or not.

Thus although he enumerates features of landscape or person, he selects and arranges details both in relationship to a frame—his stanza—and in relationship to his allegorical romance. He is prepared to give ten stanzas to portraying Belphoebe (2.3.21–31) because he considers her beauty and chastity to be worth it; he gives just two stanzas to the description of her paradise because allegorically it is important only as her setting, as amplifying her beauty. In limiting his elaborate set pieces, Spenser is trying to steer a course between narrative as a refined, but still casual, folk art and a more or less affected aestheticism, such as we may find in *Muiopotmos*.

Though all the narrative of *The Faerie Queene* is "garnished," there are degrees of ornateness. When he is not narrating but "illustrating," or making more vivid, he can produce a passage that seems pure decoration:

> Looke how the crowne, which Ariadne wore
> Upon her yvory forehead that same day
> That Theseus her unto his bridale bore,
> When the bold Centaures made that bloudy fray
> With the fierce Lapithes, which did them dismay,
> Being now placed in the firmament,
> Through the bright heaven doth her beams display,
> And is unto the starres an ornament,
> Which round about her move in order excellent.
>
> (6.10.13)

There are the usual references to beautiful things: ivory, crown, stars, brightness, orderly movement; but the allusions to classical myth are themselves a call to wonder at the beauty of the imagination. Even the "bloudy fray" of Lapiths and Centaurs, so out of place in a stricter adherence to the traditional story of Ariadne, takes on the character of contrasting roughness, not unlike E. K.'s description of "rude thickets and craggy clifts" which lend a pleasing contrast to "the daintie lineaments of beauty." These decorative considerations are never far from Spenser's mind, although modern critics may be inclined to pay attention only to significances of another kind, such as the repetition of this beauty-violence motif in the later destruction of pastoral bliss by brigands.

But, to repeat, the decorative is the form of the symbolic in this poem; it does not subserve only aesthetic ends. Here art reflects upon itself; aestheticism is curbed by religion, at the same time as it is curbed by narrative demands. But this is only to say that Spenser's rhetoric is designed to fulfil his allegorical purpose. He means to induce the kind of concentrated attention that beauty must command, yet his conception of beauty is less Alexandrian than divine. In his view, as in that of many of his contemporaries, the proper response to all beauty, whether the work of God's hands or man's, is contemplation and wonder.

If we are at all inclined to think of *The Faerie Queene* as a world dominated by art in the sense that *Muiopotmos* is, we have only to recall that the ultimate justification for what happens in the epic is less aesthetic than a matter of the heart. A narrator who responds emotionally to events necessarily makes a contrast with the chilly embroidery of *Muiopotmos*. Now God himself judges, not in terms of aesthetic perfection but in terms of love:

> And is there care in heaven? And is there love
> In heavenly spirits to these creatures bace,
> That may compassion of their evilles move?
> There is: else much more wretched were the cace

Of men then beasts. But O th'exceeding grace
Of Highest God, that loves his creatures so,
And all his workes with mercy doth embrace,
That blessed angels he sends to and fro,
To serve to wicked man, to serve his wicked foe!

(2.8.1)

God as great artist is now subordinate to God as perfect love. If this had been true in *Muiopotmos,* there must have been more pity for the fallen butterfly; but then that poem was set in another world than that in which "He sees the little sparrows fall." While we must recognize *The Faerie Queene* as a world of art, we must also recognize the subordination of art to the higher values of love and compassion. The form of the evil ones, no matter how richly designed, cannot redeem them.

NOTES

1. Thomas Nashe, "The Anatomie of Absurditie" (1589), excerpts in G. Gregory Smith, *Elizabethan Critical Essays* (Oxford, 1904), 1:329.

2. See Madeleine Doran's comment in her *Endeavours of Art* (Madison, 1954) on the Renaissance "neglect of form in the large, its cultivation of form in the small" (p. 29). But of course the cantos, as narrative segments deriving from an oral tradition of recitation, are not intended to have the same kind of structural integrity as either the stanzas or the books.

3. See pp. 51–52.

4. Abraham Fraunce, *The Third Part of the Countess of Pembrokes Yvychurch: Entituled Amintas Dale* (London, 1592), p. 24^r.

5. See *FQ.*2.9.22, where Spenser describes the human body in terms of a divine geometry:

The frame thereof seemd partly circulare,
And part triangulare: O worke divine!
Those two the first and last proportions are;
The one imperfect, mortall, foeminine,
Th' other immortall, perfect, masculine.

6. Thomas Buoni, "A Discourse of the Author upon Beauty," in his *Problemes of Beautie,* trans. Samson Lennard (London, 1606).

7. See Hugh B. Cott, "Animal Form in Relation to Appearance," in *Aspects of Form,* ed. L. L. Whyte (1951; 2d. ed., New York, 1968), pp. 121–42.

8. Sir Philip Sidney, *The Countesse of Pembrokes Arcadia,* ed. A. Feuillerat (Cambridge, 1912), 1:13.

9. See Vasari, Preface to *Lives of the Artists,* p. 1, and Castiglione, *The Book of the Courtier,* trans. Charles S. Singleton (New York, 1959), p. 78.

10. See p. 31.

11. Cf. Chastel, *Age of Humanism,* p. 220: "It is impossible to understand anything of the Renaissance if we do not accept the current premise that adornment was art itself."

12. Buoni, "A Discourse of the Author upon Beauty," in *Problemes of Beautie.*

13. Girolamo Fracastoro, *Naugerius,* trans. Ruth Kelso (Urbana, 1924), p. 69. Cf. Castiglione, *Book of the Courtier,* pp. 343–44.

14. *The Institutio Oratoria of Quintilian,* trans. H. E. Butler (New York, 1921), VIII.iii.61.

15. Alberti, *The Architecture,* trans. James Leoni (London, 1755), VI.2, p. 113.

16. Cited in Weinberg, *History of Literary Criticism in the Italian Renaissance,* 1:95.

17. John Pope-Hennessey in his *The Portrait in the Renaissance* ([New York, 1966], p. 48) notes that the design on the sleeve is actually an impresa. It is therefore significant as well as ornamental.

18. Puttenham, *Arte,* p. 138.

19. On epic as a form of praise, see O. B. Hardison, Jr., *The Enduring Monument: A Study of the Idea of Praise in Renaissance Literary Theory and Practice* (Chapel Hill, N.C., 1962). See also Thomas H. Cain, *Praise in the Faerie Queene* (Lincoln, Nebr., 1978).

20. See Lane Cooper, "The Verbal 'Ornament' (κόσμος) in Aristotle's Art of Poetry," in *Classical and Medieval Studies in Honor of E. K. Rand* (1938; rpt. Freeport, N.Y., 1968), p. 71. Cooper refers to the names of things that delight the senses, such as the names of precious stones and words drawn from the arts, as assisting ornament. See also the *Rhetorica ad Herennium,* trans. Harry Caplan (Cambridge, Mass., 1954), IV.viii.11, where the grand style is defined: "A discourse will be composed in the Grand style if to each idea are applied the most ornate words that can be found for it, whether literal or figurative."

21. Peacham, *Compleat Gentlemen* (1634), p. 43.

22. Chastel, *Age of Humanism,* p. 220.

23. J. Huizinga, *Homo Ludens,* trans. R. F. C. Hull (London, 1948), p. 7.

24. Fracastoro, *Naugerius,* p. 69. See also Boccaccio, *On Poetry,* trans. and ed. Charles G. Osgood (Princeton, 1930), p. 104: "a thing precious for no other reason, may become so for ornament's sake."

25. Demetrius discusses the superfluous element in ornament as like "the things on which the wealthy pride themselves—cornices, triglyphs, and bands of purple. Indeed, it is in itself a mark of verbal opulence" (*On Style,* trans. Rhys Roberts [Cambridge, 1903], p. 371).

26. Erasmus, *On Copia of Words and Ideas,* trans. D. B. King and H. David Rix (Milwaukee, 1963), p. 57. Cf. Cinthio, *On Romances,* p. 143. See also Walter J. Ong, *Ramus: Method and the Decay of Dialogue* (Cambridge, Mass., 1958), p. 278: "An 'ornament' of rhetoric is also indifferently styled a 'praise'

(*laus*) or an 'honor' (*honos* or *honor*) or a 'light' (*lumen*) of words or of speech."

27. Abbot Suger, *On the Abbey Church of St. Denis and Its Art Treasures,* ed. and trans. Erwin Panofsky (Princeton, 1946), p. 67.

28. E. H. Gombrich, "Visual Metaphors of Value in Art," in *Meditations on a Hobby Horse* (London, 1963), p. 16.

29. Dolce, *Aretin,* p. 61. Cf. Roskill, *Dolce's "Aretino,"* p. 115.

30. See Michael Baxandall, *Painting and Experience in Fifteenth Century Italy* (Oxford, 1972).

31. John Milton, *Areopagitica,* in *Complete Prose Works of John Milton,* II, ed. Ernest Sirluck (New Haven, 1959), p. 555.

32. Rosemond Tuve, *Elizabethan and Metaphysical Imagery* (Chicago, 1947), p. 121.

33. Cited in Weinberg, *History of Literary Criticism in the Italian Renaissance,* 2:664.

34. These passages from *Arcadia,* 260 and 70b, are cited in the notes to Hoyt H. Hudson's edition of John Hoskins, *Directions for Speech and Style,* p. 59.

35. Epistle prefixed to *The Shepheardes Calender.* Cf. Wind, *Pagan Mysteries of the Renaissance,* pp. 86–88, on *discordia concors.*

36. Francesco Colonna, *Hypnerotomachia: The Strife of Loue in a Dreame,* Book I, trans. Sir Robert Dallington (1592), p. 45^{v}.

37. Ibid., pp. 51$^{\text{r-v}}$.

38. Sidney, *Apology for Poetry,* p. 138. In *The Merchant of Venice,* Shakespeare has Bassanio make a similar rejection of ornament as disguise: "The world is still deceiv'd with ornament" (III.ii.74).

39. Hoskins, *Directions for Speech and Style,* p. 7.

40. Quintilian, *Institutio Oratoria,* VIII.v.34.

41. Alberti, *On Painting,* pp. 75–76.

42. See Rosemary Freeman, *English Emblem Books* (1948; rpt. New York, 1966), p. 94. For a fuller treatment of the interaction between ornament and symbol in the visual arts, see E. H. Gombrich, "Designs as Signs," in his *Sense of Order* (Ithaca, 1979), pp. 217–50.

43. See Ida Langdon, *Milton's Theory of Poetry and Fine Art* (1924; rpt. New York, 1965), pp. 31–32, on Milton's general lack of interest in minute descriptions of fine workmanship.

44. Lessing held that the parts did not coalesce to form a picture for the imagination. See *Laocoon,* trans. William A. Steel (London, 1930), pp. 74–79.

45. Dolce, *Aretin,* p. 111. Cf. Roskill, *Dolce's "Aretino,"* p. 131.

CHAPTER 5

Image as Expression

I

In *The Faerie Queene,* everything coheres: the building-block conception of structure, the decorative form, the expressiveness of objects and scenes. One implies the other, and therefore we cannot ask why Spenser does this or that, without questioning why he does everything. Drawing as he does upon an already existing vocabulary of forms and motifs, he follows a doctrine of expressiveness that is remote from modern artistic concerns. Instead of expressing his own inner life, it is the special task of the Renaissance poet to give true and beautiful expression to the characteristic features of things, persons, nature, even concepts. But this expressiveness can never be an end in itself, since everything is to be presented in such a way as to affect the audience. Such an essentially oratorical view of expression required, above all, the ability to choose among forms that lay to hand and the power to infuse them with new life and beauty.

To move from the notion of images as a method of beautifying the poet's style to consideration of their affective purpose is to adopt a slightly different perspective but not necessarily to single out a new class of images. Although Puttenham speaks of figures as serving a purpose "either of

beautie or of efficacie," by which he means that the one "en-
forceth the sence," while the other "urges affection,"[1] in
practice the two ends are met by the same images in the allegory of *The Faerie Queene.* That is to say, the pictorial illusion which the poet attempted to achieve in narration by his
use of descriptive schemes is both ornamental, or beautiful,
in design and efficacious, or moving, in effect. We may note,
for example, that in Henry Peacham's definition of efficacy,
pictorial illusion and ornament are both implied: "*Efficacie* is
a power of speech, which representeth a thing after an excellent manner: neither by bare words onely, but by presenting
to our minds the liuely *Idaea's* or formes of things so truely,
as if we saw them with our eyes."[2] The separation between
ornament and persuasion is one that exists only in critical
analysis: their ends appear to differ, in that ornament is self-
sufficient and inert, whereas persuasion, based on the moving
power of images, works upon an audience to effect action.
But in the practice of Renaissance literature, both beauty and
efficacy are achieved by the same rhetorical methods.[3]

Now according to Sidney, the didactic aim of poetry could
only be fulfilled if an image was planted in the reader's imagination, to grow there. But his use of this organic metaphor
transforms our previous view of the image as decorative object into something more compelling, although not necessarily identical with the Neoplatonic emphasis on the image as a
source of higher knowledge.[4] Rather, what the didactic view
of the poetic image suggests is something like the role of
images in memory theory. Certainly the type of memory images described in the *Ad Herennium* have much of the emotional character of Spenser's images:

> We ought, then, to set up images of a kind that can
> adhere longest in the memory. And we shall do so if we
> establish likenesses as striking as possible; if we set up

images that are not many or vague, but doing something; if we assign to them exceptional beauty or singular ugliness; if we dress some of them with crowns or purple cloaks, for example, so that the likeness may be more distinct to us; or if we somewhat disfigure them as by introducing one stained with blood or soiled with mud or smeared with red paint, so that its form is more striking, or by assigning certain comic effects to our images, for that, too, will ensure our remembering them more readily. The things we easily remember when they are real we likewise remember without difficulty when they are figments if they have been carefully delineated. But this will be essential—again and again to run over rapidly in the mind all the original backgrounds in order to refresh the images.[5]

We shall be observing some of these striking effects in Spenser's images; meanwhile, it is enough to note that there is a reciprocal relationship between memory and imagination: the memory holds what the judgment selects from the imagination as worthy of remembering, and, in turn, the imagination can contemplate its own creations in the memory. As Andreas Laurentius explains, "man hath the libertie to imagine what he listeth, and although there be no present object, yet it taketh out of the treasurie, which is the memorie whatsoeuer may content it."[6]

What will "content" the imagination, it seems, are "adjuncts" or "accidents," such as the "crowns or purple cloaks" or the smearing of a person with blood, mud, or red paint. The importance of adjuncts is also stressed in the rhetorical theory of illustration or amplification, which has already been examined in Chapter 3 as "the counterfait representation." For example, in treating the logical place "Subject and Adjuncts," Abraham Fraunce explains how a person may be characterized by such a personal attribute as laughing, or how an object may be identified by a common quality, such as a stone by its whiteness.[7] Since the real subject or substance is invisible to our bodily eyes, we need such "accidents" as these to perceive it, both in real life and in description. So familiar is Spenser with this principle that he almost makes use of "accidents" as if they were the kind of attributes used in medieval or Renaissance painting to identify saints or mythological figures.[8] Consider his initial characterization of Samient by her fear:

> Yet fled she fast, and both them farre outwent,
> Carried with wings of feare, like fowle aghast,
> With locks all loose, and rayment all torent;
> And ever as she rode, her eye was backeward bent.
>
> (5.8.4)

The image has the emblematic quality of providing an unambiguous definition by means of a few visual details, reinforced by auditory touches. The reiterated breathless *f*'s of the description in the first line are linked in the second line with a metaphor, "wings of feare," and a simile, "like fowle aghast"; then adjuncts which become more and more specific are introduced with three additional alliterations—*l, r, b*—the liquid sounds *l* and *r* suggesting lack of control, the plosive *b* conveying by sound the fixity of the backward-turning eye. Together, the sounds suggest both her headlong course and the paralysis of her emotional state. This carefully patterned arrangement of words and details culminates in the alexandrine with its final decisive detail of the backward-looking eye, so indicative of the fearful mind. The image is fashioned to remain in the mind as both striking in its details and decorative in its construction.

In depicting an emotionally expressive figure, Spenser has followed the precepts laid down from classical times on the artist's need to study the characteristics of all the human emotions for the sake of verisimilitude in narrative. Thus Aristotle in his *Rhetoric* had said: "And in narrating, employ the traits of emotion. Use the symptoms familiar to all." He gives as an example the passage from the *Odyssey* where we hear of Eurycleia's reaction to Penelope's reference to the lost Odysseus: "So she spake; but the old woman buried her face in her hands." Aristotle comments: "It is the right touch: people beginning to weep put their hands to their eyes." This essential rightness in portraying emotional reactions also implies the "good will and kindliness" of the speaker and therefore confirms the audience's faith in him.[9] Although it is not fashionable nowadays to refer to, or believe in, the unchanging human heart, it was on the assumption of a general human consistency in the expression of emotion that most of the art and literature of the past was based.

Tasso makes explicit the prevailing attitude of the Renaissance: "Now what is in itself is always so, for all the changes of custom. Hence cannibalism will always be thought savage although it was customary in some nations; modesty always has and will be a virtue, even if Spartan women were less than chaste. . . . What is suitable to the ethos of the boy, the old man, the rich, powerful, poor, noble, or ignoble man in one era is suitable in every era; otherwise Aristotle would not have dealt with the matter, since he professes to teach only what pertains to art."[10] This is the kind of assumption that lies behind references to decorum in the depiction of character, or, equally, references to the means of making an image expressive. Tasso is referring, for example, to Aristotle's treatment of the qualities of old men, such as avarice, timidity, slowness, and so on. But the descriptive schemata emphasize and rely upon the categorization not only of human beings but of all experience. Hence, we often find descriptions labeled by Renaissance critics or annotators as if they belonged to particular types—for example, Harington's comment on one of Ariosto's descriptions: "a description of an effeminate courtier," or "a description of the assault of a towne well defended."[11] And, as Tasso indicates, particular emotional responses are associated with all manner of descriptions, in accordance with values that are fundamentally rational and humane.

Since poetry was to appeal more strongly to the passions than oratory, it was accepted that a classification such as happy and sad feelings might serve as a schematic view of the province of poetry. For this reason the great antitheses of Spenser's poetry are not antitheses of ideas but of feelings. He can find a thousand patterns in the universe for illustrations of the universal contrasts of feeling; he can use the rose and its thorn, or he can use day and night, or even concepts such as mutability and permanence; but underlying them all is a sense of what is pleasing or displeasing to the human heart. He seems to agree with Bacon that "pleasure and pain are to the particular affections, as light is to particular colors."[12] It is this antithesis that dominates his imagery, along with its corollary of sympathy and antipathy.

That these simple polarities should govern the choice of expression is indicated by theorists writing on both literature and painting. Wilson, for example, emphasizes the importance of choosing the right expressions to produce in an audience "a stirring or forsing of the minde, either to desire, or else to detest and loth any thing, more vehemently then by nature we are commonly wont to doe. . . . Neither onely are wee moued with those things, which wee thinke either hurtfull, or profitable for our selues, but also we reioyse, we be sorie, or wee pittie an other mans happe. . . . In mouing affections, and stirring the Iudges to be greeued, the waight of the matter must be set forth, as though they sawe it plaine before their eyes."[13] Dolce sees in this power to affect the basis for the critical analogy between poet and painter: "the

figures should affect the minds of the observers; some dis-
turbing them, others allaying that tumult; some moving them
to pity, others to disdain or wrath, according to the nature of
the history represented; otherwise the painter may fairly
conclude that he has done nothing; for this is the grand result
of all his other excellencies. The same may be observed of
the Poet, the Historian, and the Orator; for if what they write
or recite wants this power, it is destitute of all life and
spirit."[14] And this life and spirit is exactly the crux of the
whole dilemma for the artist who uses emotive formulas: how
is he to infuse them with life so that they will affect the reader
or the viewer?

If for the painter it had become necessary to make his
schema match life by close observation,[15] the poet needed
rather to have an imagination readily stirred to form images
in keeping with traditional expressive formulas; he needed,
as well, a capacity to bring these images before the minds of
others by means of words. Perhaps the mysterious way in
which the poet or orator must respond to his own interior
images in order to make others see them can most easily be
understood in terms of what a good actor will feel when he
portrays a dramatic character. In *The Faerie Queene,* efficacy
largely depends upon the dramatic ability of the narrator, for
it is he who identifies and conveys the expressive quality of
person, place, work of art, and so on, as though they spoke
even when they are silent. We see the character of everything
as he presents it to us, whether beautiful or ugly, sympathetic
or antipathetic.

As the ancient critics, including Longinus, Horace, and
Quintilian, all noted, there is no substitute for genuine emotion on the part of the speaker if he is to move his listeners.
The question of how this emotion was to be generated was
difficult to answer, but Quintilian and Longinus talk about
the power of the imagination to conjure up images which in

turn will move the audience. The most detailed discussion is in Quintilian, who refers to the daydreams and hallucinations to which people are subject and how they may be used. "It is," he says, "the man who is really sensitive to such impressions who will have the greatest power over the emotions." Then, as an example of how vividness of depiction may be secured, he says:

> I am complaining that a man has been murdered. Shall I not bring before my eyes all the circumstances which it is reasonable to imagine must have occurred in such a connection? Shall I not see the assassin burst suddenly from his hiding-place, the victim tremble, cry for help, beg for mercy, or turn to run? Shall I not see the fatal blow delivered and the stricken body fall? Will not the blood, the deathly pallor, the groan of agony, the death-rattle, be indelibly impressed upon my mind?
>
> From such impressions arises that enargia which Cicero calls illumination and actuality, which makes us seem not so much to narrate as to exhibit the actual scene, while our emotions will be no less actively stirred than if we were present at the actual occurrence.[16]

He alludes to Virgil's source of inspiration in such visions, and Renaissance critics would sometimes refer to Dante in similar terms as first "seeing" his visions and then describing them.[17] The whole rhetorical concept of *enargeia,* or vivid representation, thus seems to have had its counterpart in a psychological theory, although then, as now, the actual workings of the imagination were something of a mystery. It is tantalizing to read such a standard Renaissance definition of *enargeia* or *evidentia* as Erasmus's: "We use this whenever, for the sake of amplifying, adorning or pleasing, we do not state a thing simply, but set it forth to be viewed as though portrayed in color on a tablet, so that it may seem that we have painted, not narrated, and that the reader has seen, not read. We will be able to do this well if we first conceive a mental picture of the subject with all its attendant circumstances. Then we should so portray it in words and fitting figures that it is as clear and graphic as possible to the reader. In this sort of excellence all the poets are eminent but especially Homer."[18] But there is no doubt that *enargeia* involved the fantasy or imagination of the poet, on the one hand—that is, "making likenesses with the mind alone"[19]—and power, by means of words, over the emotions and passions of the audience, on the other hand.

Certainly Spenser, as well as Homer, Virgil, or Dante, must have had his imagination stirred by the inner visions which his allegorical narrative required, no matter what their original sources in iconography. That such a figure as his Despair conforms to an emotive formula may be illustrated by a comparison between his description and the way Leonardo recommends that a man in despair be depicted. First, Leonardo: "You will show the man in despair stabbing himself with a knife, having torn his garments with his hands. Let one of his hands be shown in the act of tearing open his wound, he himself standing on his feet, but with his legs somewhat bent, and his whole body also bent toward the ground; his hair torn and disarrayed."[20]

Now Spenser:

> That darkesome cave they enter, where they find
> That cursed man, low sitting on the ground,
> Musing full sadly in his sullein mind:
> His griesie lockes, long growen and unbound,
> Disordred hong about his shoulders round,
> And hid his face; through which his hollow eyne
> Lookt deadly dull, and stared as astound;
> His raw-bone cheekes, through penurie and pine,
> Were shronke into his jawes, as he did never dyne.

His garment nought but many ragged clouts,
With thornes together pind and patched was,
The which his naked sides he wrapt abouts;
And him beside there lay upon the gras
A dreary corse, whose life away did pas,
All wallowd in his own yet luke-warme blood,
That from his wound yet welled fresh, alas!
In which a rusty knife fast fixed stood,
And made an open passage for the gushing flood.

$$(1.9.35-36)$$

Although Spenser's Despair is not identical to Leonardo's in
his features, he shares the torn garments, the disordered hair,
and even a posture that reflects his state of mind: Leonardo
has "his whole body bent toward the ground," while Spenser
has him "low sitting on the ground." Then, too, though
Spenser's Despair never stabs himself as Leonardo's does,
rather hanging himself after losing Red Cross as a prey, still
the knight lying beside him has blood welling from a wound.
It seems obvious that Spenser and Leonardo were drawing
upon a common tradition for the representation of such
figures; and although the one must use words to call up "attendant circumstances," the other, pen or paint to show bodily gesture, both assume a similar classification of feelings.
Accuracy in adhering to these emotive categories was considered so important that to deviate was to "whollie pervert
the order of things, confounding the beauty of Histories,
whether they be fables, or other inventions which are to be
painted."[21] So Lomazzo cautions the painter to respect human psychology as tradition had analyzed it.

Similarly, the poet, in attempting to give the illusion of
reality, has to respect universal standards of judgment. These
standards are most easily discerned in Spenser's use of adjectives. In themselves, they are unequivocal: "gentle mayd,"
"dreary night." They become equivocal only when the con-

text by other means puts us on our guard for possible ironic overtones. When the rhetoricians define epithet as "a figure or forme of speech, which ioyneth Adiectiues to those Sub-stantiues to whom they do properly belong, and that either to praise or dispraise, to amplifie, or extenuate,"[22] they are indicating that the function of adjectives is to evaluate. But the phrase "to whom they do properly belong" suggests the principle of decorum as well: "what fits places, times, and persons." Just as there was thought to be a speech and a behavior befitting every type of person in a poem or play, so for everyone and every object that could be named, there was an appropriate epithet. No doubt there is something primitive in this habit of attaching an adjective to every noun as if it were an identification tag.[23] But Spenser's use of such epithets shows how he both imitates the earlier oral tradition of heroic poetry and transforms it in accordance with his own purpose. His epithets are used too self-consciously to be either mere line-filling words or simply a means of identification; instead, they subtly shape the reader's response by emphasizing the narrator's judgment, as well as the expressive qualities of things.

A consistently anthropocentric point of view is implied in this use of adjectives. The praising and blaming assume that there are fixed standards of virtue and beauty and that concepts themselves can be praised or blamed according to the way human beings traditionally view them. The stock image, as Spenser uses it, is informed with a conventional sensibility designed to elicit a stock response—the "correct" emotion for any given occasion. It may be sympathy for a good knight, antipathy for a bad, or pity for the victim and hatred for the oppressor, or cheerfulness at daybreak and melancholy at nightfall. If trees are described as "loftie" or a shore as "sandie," these adjectives allude to nature in relation to the human being. Everything in the outer world is expressive, because man is bound in a unity with this outer world. Since, for example, man's life has its seasons, Colin Clout's comparison between the outer world and his inner world in the January and December eclogues of *The Shepheardes Calender* is less symptomatic of the "pathetic fallacy" than suggestive of the oneness which includes both man and nature. In this context, the physiognomic characteristics of nature are bound to seem as expressive as people's eyebrows or hands.[24]

Consider the way Una and Red Cross "read" the character of the grove where they take shelter from a storm.

> Enforst to seek some covert nigh at hand,
> A shadie grove not farr away they spide,
> That promist ayde the tempest to withstand:
> Whose loftie trees, yclad with sommers pride,
> Did spred so broad, that heavens light did hide,
> Not perceable with power of any starre:
> And all within were pathes and alleis wide,
> With footing worne, and leading inward farr:
> Faire harbour that them seemes, so in they entred ar.
>
> (1.1.7)

The essential character of the grove is first established: "That promist ayde the tempest to withstand." Here is the elemental note, a primal significance of groves. And every detail of the description serves to emphasize this view, whether it is the "star-proof" branching of the trees, or the multitude of worn footpaths suggestive of a "faire harbour."[25] It is a grove interpreted—incorrectly, as it proves—under the stress of particular human needs. Another grove may provide shelter for a knight from the sun, instead of from a tempest; he rests

> foreby a fountaine syde,
> Disarmed all of yron-coted plate,
> And by his side his steed the grassy forage ate.
>
> He feeds upon the cooling shade, and bayes
> His sweatie forehead in the breathing wynd,

Which through the trembling leaves full gently playes,
Wherein the chearefull birds of sundry kynd
Doe chaunt sweet musick, to delight his mynd.

(1.7.2 – 3)

In these images there is practically no revelation, no inevitability of words, but there is an inevitability of feeling. The contrasts are the fundamental ones of cool shade, breathing wind, and bird song, on the one hand, and the sweaty forehead of the knight, on the other hand. Each noun has its expressive qualities intensified by an epithet, so that everything may "speak"; and because, as everywhere in the poem, the humanly perceived quality of things is represented, the total effect is of a stable, identifiable reality.

So pervasive is this affective emphasis that no rhetorical device escapes it. The epic similes are a striking instance. Detached as they are from the narrative proper, they show almost in the abstract the operation of a favorite principle of Spenser's. In order to assert the universality of a feeling, he most often appeals to the pleasure-pain principle of which Bacon spoke. These imagistic contrasts tell their own tale of conventional sensibility: the rose and its thorn are not more conventionally symbolic than the withered tree and the fruitful one, sunshine and clouds, golden foil and baser metal. Such contrasts also appear everywhere in Shakespeare's plays—in Prince Hal's soliloquy, for example, at the end of the first act of *Henry IV, Part I*—but are turned to the revelation of character. In Spenser, on the other hand, they remain descriptive absolutes, reminding the reader of a familiar world of sensation through the voice of a speaker whose task it is to present the naive response to experience.

Even the conventional descriptions of time, known to rhetoricians as *cronographiae,* can take on the emotional tenor of a situation. Spenser is not confined to one formula: night may be the cloak of evil, a sleepy season, a beautiful spectacle;

dawn may be a time to renew activity, an ironic contrast to man's troubled mind, or, like night, a beautiful spectacle. There are actually innumerable ways of adjusting the temper of the *cronographiae* to the dramatic situation, and the use of periphrasis in many of these descriptions is like a living illustration of Longinus's words: "That periphrasis contributes to the sublime, no one, I fancy, would question. Just as in music what we call ornament enhances the beauty of the main theme, so periphrasis often chimes in with the literal expression of our meaning and gives it a far richer note."[26] The first two cantos of Book III, each dominated by a night scene, show some of the possible variations. The *cronographia* that introduces the night scene between Britomart and Malecasta uses an elaborate periphrasis:

> By this th' eternall lampes, wherewith high Jove
> Doth light the lower world, were halfe yspent,
> And the moist daughters of huge Atlas strove
> Into the ocean deepe to drive their weary drove.
>
> (3.1.57)

Coming as it does at the end of a stanza, it has also the benefit of the drawn-out alexandrine to help emphasize the lateness of the hour and the weariness of all the guests. Some of this weariness, it is worth noting, remains in the diminishing *cronographia* which marks the coming of dawn, to remind us that this night has not been spent with profit to either body or soul:

> So, eareley, ere the grosse earthes gryesy shade
> Was all disperst out of the firmament,
> They tooke their steeds, and forth upon their journey
>   went.   (3.1.67)

Using no mythological allusions, the subdued tone furnishes a quiet close to this particular action and to the whole canto.

In the second canto, the night scene begins far less dramatically, with a restrained personification:

> So soone as Night had with her pallid hew
> Defaste the beautie of the shyning skye,
> And reft from men the worldes desired vew,
> She with her nourse adowne to sleepe did lye.
>
> (3.2.28)

The interest of this scene lies, not in overt action, but in the feminine tenderness which requires the concealment of night before revealing itself to anyone. The setting, though essential, must be established as unostentatiously as possible; the images are quiet, barely mentioning such things as the "warm bed" and "dronken lamp that down in the oyl did steepe." Morning, too, comes with no fanfare, but with perhaps a touch of irony, considering the heaviness of two hearts:

> Earely the morrow next, before that day
> His joyous face did to the world revele,
> They both uprose.
>
> (3.2.48)

Spenser is fond of using his *cronographiae* for this kind of delicate irony when it is convenient to do so.

Simply by examining all the *cronographiae* of Book III, one could gain a fair sense of the subtlety with which he makes conventional expressions convey affective tone. When he wishes, he can leave one of these descriptions as purely conventional as he does in Canto 8 when the Squire of Dames suggests to his companions that they seek shelter for the night at Malbecco's castle:

> But sith the sunne now ginnes to slake his beames
> In deawy vapours of the westerne mayne,
> And lose the teme out of his weary wayne,
> Mote not mislike you also to abate

> Your zealous hast, till morrow next againe
> Doth light of heven and strength of men relate.
>
>   (3.8.51)

Here the periphrasis seems to be merely part of a polite form
of address; it does not at once announce a dramatic action.
But early in the next canto, when the group of knights has
been refused admittance into the castle, the fact of night and
the accompanying storm become sufficiently important to
require nothing beyond adjectival emphasis:

>   the night was forward spent,
> And the faire welkin, fowly overcast,
> Gan blowen up a bitter stormy blast,
> With showere and hayle.
>
>   (3.9.11)

Indeed, the passing hours make themselves felt with almost
relentless force until the critical moment when Paridell carries off Hellenore. The *cronographia* then is simple and
emphatic:

> Darke was the evening, fit for lovers stealth.
>
>   (3.10.12)

Spenser knows when a periphrasis will be dramatically effec-
tive and when it will not: the unadorned factualness of this
statement conveys the lack of sympathy for any of the pro-
tagonists. In contrast, he makes the coming of night part of
Britomart's trial at the House of Busirane, amplifying the descriptions of time in order to emphasize her heroism:

> Tho, when as chearelesse night ycovered had
> Fayre heaven with an universall cloud,
> That every wight, dismayd with darkenes sad,
> In silence and in sleepe themselves did shrowd,
> She heard a shrilling trompet sound alowd.
>
>   (3.12.1)

It is interesting to note how the dull *k* sound gives way to the somnolent *s* sound, but then how this same *s* sound in the last line is transformed into a cry to action. Nothing more tellingly demonstrates Spenser's concern to make the conventional expressive than his handling of time descriptions, for here, if anywhere, one might expect a perfunctoriness in keeping with the static nature of these formulas.

II

By showing us good and evil in the clear-cut terms of our own sympathies and antipathies, Spenser has fulfilled the first duty of the moralist, but he has also followed the rhetorical principle that description has the purpose of praising or blaming. The medieval precedent is enunciated by Faral: "dans toute la littérature du moyen âge, la description ne vise que très rarement à peindre objectivement les personnes et les choses et . . . elle soit toujours dominée par une intention affective qui oscille entre la louange et la critique."[27] Yet within the general pattern of praise and blame in *The Faerie Queene* there are nuances of style that qualify our judgment of what is presented. A subtle decorum governs the method of description, influencing our response in ways that we may not be conscious of. How, for example, does Spenser convey the difference between the false simplicity of Archimago's pose as a hermit and the true simplicity of the palmer? The conventional details of the palmer's appearance have already been noted in Chapter 3: the black attire, the hair "all hoarie gray," the staff to support his aged steps. The details are fewer than those given for Archimago's version of the hermit:

> At length they chaunst to meet upon the way
> An aged sire, in long blacke weedes yclad,

His feete all bare, his beard all hoarie gray,
And by his belt his booke he hanging had;
Sober he seemde, and very sagely sad,
And to the ground his eyes were lowly bent,
Simple in shew, and voide of malice bad,
And all the way he prayed as he went,
And often knockt his brest, as one that did repent.

                                                      (1.1.29)

Both hermits are described by the adjectives "sober" and "sage," but the description is made more emphatic for Archimago by lengthening the adjective "sage" to "very sagely sad." Another addition to the portrait of the false hermit is the line "Simple in shew, and voide of malice bad," in place of the more cautious "And if by lookes one may the mind aread" for the palmer. Finally, Archimago prays and knocks his breast as he walks along, whereas the palmer simply leads Guyon at a slow, steady pace. Together the variations in these two portraits suggest how Spenser, using similar conventional elements, will habitually guide the reader's judgment in distinguishing between the good and the seeming good. One method is to exaggerate features in the evil person or place. It has already been remarked that the beauties of the Bower of Bliss are overdone, a clue to the falsity of this apparent paradise. Similarly, Archimago overplays his part, as people are prone to do when they are chiefly concerned with appearances.

Another example of how Spenser can use the same conventions to describe both the good and the evil may be found in the parallels between the House of Pride and Mercilla's palace. Both of them are "stately" and both are adorned with gold to outshine the sky. Here is the description of the House of Pride:

A stately pallace built of squared bricke,
Which cunningly was without morter laid,

> Whose wals were high, but nothing strong nor thick,
> And golden foile all over them displaid,
> That purest skye with brightnesse they dismaid:
> High lifted up were many loftie towres,
> And goodly galleries far over laid,
> Full of faire windowes and delightful bowres;
> And on the top a diall told the timely howres.

(1.4.4)

And Mercilla's palace:

> The gentle knights rejoyced much to heare
> The prayses of that prince so manifold,
> And passing litle further, commen were
> Where they a stately pallace did behold,
> Of pompous show, much more then she had told;
> With many towres and tarras mounted hye,
> And all their tops bright glistering with gold,
> That seemed to outshine the dimmed skye,
> And with their brightnesse daz'd the straunge beholders
> eye. (5.9.21)

The details given for the House of Pride suggest deception and weakness—the "cunningly" laid bricks, the lack of
strength in the walls—as well as pleasure: the "goodly galleries," "faire windows," "delightful bowres." But these inti-
mations of sensual pleasure become ominously linked to time
by the reference in the last line to the dial on top of the
palace. The next stanza picks up these faint warnings to make
them explicit in the description of the weak foundations. In
this context, the use of gold for the House of Pride becomes
profane in contrast with its sacred use in the adornment of
Mercilla's palace. A similar contrast prevails in the descriptions of Lucifera and Mercilla which immediately follow.[28]
But these last examples only reiterate the point made in the
previous chapter, that the expressive value of ornament depends upon the context in which it appears.

Besides the beauty associated with allusions to gold, jewels, and other precious things, there is also the beauty recognized by rhetoricians as deriving from smooth, sweet rhythms. Spenser's care in suiting style to subject, or, in the words of Tasso echoing Demetrius, in making "words follow concepts,"[29] is apparent in the description of Amphitrite, Neptune's queen. This image has both the subject matter of beauty—Greek myth—and the lovely words and flowing rhythms, with unemphatic alliteration added in the last lines as a kind of grace note:

> And by his side his queene with coronall,
> Faire Amphitrite, most divinely faire,
> Whose yvorie shoulders weren covered all,
> As with a robe, with her owne silver haire,
> And deckt with pearles, which th' Indian seas for her
>   prepaire.   (4.11.11)

There is a minimum of tension because here the poet is free to describe a figure from the beautiful world of myth and need not point a moral.

In Spenser's mind, this world of myth seems to call for a more ornate style than, say, the beauty of the pastoral realm. In the description of Pastorella as Calidore first sees her, her adornments are themselves in keeping with the decorum of the lowly style:

>   a faire damzell, which did weare a crowne
> Of sundry flowres, with silken ribbands tyde,
> Yclad in home-made greene that her owne hands had dyde.

> Upon a litle hillocke she was placed
> Higher then all the rest, and round about
> Environed with a girland, goodly graced,
> Of lovely lasses, and them all without
> The lustie shepheard swaynes sate in a rout,
> The which did pype and sing her prayses dew.

                                                   (6.9.7–8)

Rustic simplicity, with its moral connotations, precludes the elegant language of the Amphitrite description. One might contrast the description of Calidore's vision of the graces, in which the word "girlond" is again used to describe the circle gathered around the "precious gemme," but in that passage the whole style is so much more elevated that we can at once see that Spenser has taken us out of the pastoral realm into something which is closer to the mythological:

> All they without were raunged in a ring,
> And danced round; but in the midst of them
> Three other ladies did both daunce and sing,
> The whilest the rest them round about did hemme,
> And like a girlond did in compasse stemme:
> And in the middest of those same three was placed
> Another damzell, as a precious gemme
> Amidst a ring most richly well enchaced,
> That with her goodly presence all the rest much graced.
>
> (6.10.12)

At the center of this dancing ring is the "precious gemme," Colin Clout's beloved, illustrating, as it were, Gracián's definition of grace as "the ornament of ornament."[30] The starry crown of Ariadne, introduced as a simile in the next stanza, splendidly confirms the value both of ornament and of grace: "And is unto the starres an ornament, / Which round about her move in order excellent."

But almost by definition, all moments of beauty in the poem—all moments, that is, of total harmony, in which the verse seems to sing—are fleeting. We are drawn relentlessly back into the struggle, much as Calidore is. Perhaps of all the battles in *The Faerie Queene,* the one which most vividly expresses the cruelty and arrogance of a pagan opponent is that between Prince Arthur and the Souldan. It begins with the dreaded appearance of the Souldan upon "a charret hye, / With yron wheeles and hookes arm'd dreadfully, / And

drawne of cruell steedes, which he had fed / With flesh of
men." There follow two stanzas contrasting this tyrant with
Arthur, first in their appearance:

> So forth he came, all in a cote of plate,
> Burnisht with bloudie rust; whiles on the greene
> The Briton Prince him readie did awayte,
> In glistering armes right goodly well beseene,
> That shone as bright as doth the heaven sheene.
>
> (5.8.29)

The difference in the appearance of their armor—"bloudie
rust" contrasted with "glistering armes"—symbolizes the difference between their characters, which is described next:

> Thus goe they both together to their geare,
> With like fierce minds, but meanings different:
> For the proud Souldan, with presumpteous cheare,
> And contenance sublime and insolent,
> Sought onely slaughter and avengement:
> But the brave Prince for honour and for right,
> Gainst tortious powre and lawlesse regiment,
> In the behalfe of wronged weake did fight:
> More in his causes truth he trusted then in might.
>
> (5.8.30)

It may be noted that the adjectives and nouns associated with
the Souldan are two- or three-syllabled: "presumpteous,"
"countenance sublime and insolent," "slaughter and avenge-
ment," "tortious powre and lawlesse regiment." The words
that describe Arthur, on the other hand, are simple and predominantly monosyllabic: "for honour and for right"; he
fights "in the behalfe of wronged weake" and trusts "More in
his causes truth . . . then in might." Thus not only do the
pictorial details of their armor express their characters but
the abstract words used to identify these spiritual differences
also help to build the pictures of opposing types.

In the ensuing battle, since the Souldan's horses have the chief part, the expressive quality of the verse is concentrated on speed:

> Oft drew the Prince unto his charret nigh,
> In hope some stroke to fasten on him neare;
> But he was mounted in his seat so high,
> And his wingfooted coursers him did beare
> So fast away, that ere his readie speare
> He could advance, he farre was gone and past.
> Yet still he him did follow every where,
> And followed was of him likewise full fast,
> So long as in his steedes the flaming breath did last.
>
> (5.8.33)

For Spenser the consonant *f* is often used to suggest speed; it is used for example in the descriptions of the flight of Florimell and Samient. But the words here also suggest violent action, so that the total effect is a masterly evocation of the struggle of man against fierce horses. A mythological simile follows, drawing a parallel between the Souldan's death under the hooves of his own horses and the death of Hippolytus:

> Like as the cursed sonne of Theseus,
> That, following his chace in dewy morne,
> To fly his stepdames love outrageous,
> Of his own steedes was all to peeces torne,
> And his faire limbs left in the woods forlorne;
> That for his sake Diana did lament,
> And all the wooddy nymphes did wayle and mourne:
> So was this Souldan rapt and all to-rent,
> That of his shape appear'd no litle moniment.
>
> (5.8.43)

But the parallel also includes contrast between Hippolytus, whose death was mourned by a goddess and by nymphs, and the Souldan, of whose shape "appear'd no litle moniment." Once the Souldan is dead, beauty can return, and the rhythms change to ones befitting the "wooddy nymphes"—a far cry from the bloodstained armor.

There are also less violent methods of correction in *The Faerie Queene.* When Serena and Timias must be purged of their ills by the hermit, the language becomes as plain and blunt as he himself is:

> Small was his house, and like a little cage,
> For his owne turne, yet inly neate and clene,
> Deckt with green boughes and flowers gay beseene.
> Therein he them full faire did entertaine,
> Not with such forged showes, as fitter beene
> For courting fooles, that curtesies would faine,
> But with entire affection and appearaunce plaine.
>
> (6.5.38)

For Spenser can eschew beauty when he wants to and follow the "graver Muses" that fit his serious purpose; he makes no mistake about what is "writt, in stone / With bloody letter by the hand of God." Nor does he miss seeing the reward from following the steep little path. If Hermogenes knew nought of holiness, as George Herbert says,[31] Spenser knew how to describe the companionship of angels:

> As he thereon stood gazing, he might see
> The blessed angels to and fro descend
> From highest heaven, in gladsome companee,
> And with great joy into that citty wend,
> As commonly as frend does with his frend.
>
> (1.10.56)

The simple style comes into its own as not merely the style befitting romance but the style befitting religious vision—at once exalted and humble.

If the limits of expression are determined by the overriding principle of decorum[32]—that is, the appropriateness of style to concept—what does this mean for Spenser's poem as a whole? As we examine the parts, we discover a decorum of the part, a variety of styles to match the variety of characters and events. But clearly, something must hold all this together, for if epic, like the painter's *istoria,* should encompass the whole range of human life, there must still be a unity to the composition. That unity, as I have already suggested, derives from Spenser's seriousness of purpose; this alone can explain both the splendor and the simplicity of his style, qualities not so much opposed as one might think. They equally become expressions of devout feeling and take on a grandeur that can only come from "lofty thoughts." It does not take epic similes or invocations to turn this romance into epic; the weightiness is already there without these ornaments.

But more than weightiness, the style of the whole poem implies a mystery or a cloudy revelation. We are confronted with the paradox of the intense clarity of the image and the mystery of its significance, for even the allegory and the personifying names for characters do not dispel the mystery of implying so much that cannot be said directly. The dark conceit cannot but dignify the childish tales of old romance. But all this is presented not as mystery but as plain truth; where mystery is directly presented, as in the dream of Britomart, an interpreter-priest is called in to explain. Yet the inexplicable images of her dream in the Temple of Isis—the transformations of attire and storm and animal behavior—are only slightly more dreamlike and mysterious than the ordinary images of the narrative. Out of awe for the symbol, the language must be solemn:

> There did appeare unto her heavenly spright
> A wondrous vision. . . .

> All sodainely she saw transfigured
> Her linnen stole to robe of scarlet red,
> And moone-like mitre to a crowne of gold.
>
> $(5.7.12-13)$

Intensity comes not from the tumult of passions but from looking intently both at the visible appearance and at the invisible significance. In short, any reference to the expressiveness of Spenser's images must take into account the limits imposed by his religious perspective, as well as by his epic genre.

On the surface, such a remark as Tasso's, that decorum is to virtue as beauty is to health,[33] does no more than pick up the decorative connotations of the word, much as Puttenham does when he defines decorum as a "comelinesse" or "lovely conformitie." But when the high style of beauty becomes the equivalent of chivalric morality, we must concede that not only is the style the man but that the style reflects values which can find no other form of expression. As Puttenham explains: "every mans stile is for the most part according to the matter and subject of the writer, or so ought to be, and conformable thereunto. Then againe may it be said as wel, that men doo chuse their subjects according to the mettal of their minds, and therfore a high minded man chuseth him high and lofty matter to write of."[34]

Given "the mettal" of Spenser's own mind, it becomes a particularly interesting question how he handles images of ugliness in order to make them conform to the beauty and gravity of his poem. His rhetorical purpose of course required such images as those of Envy and Detraction, or of Duessa unmasked. As Sidney noted, "Now, as in geometry the oblique must be known as well as the right, and in arithmetic the odd as well as the even, so in the actions of our life who seeth not the filthiness of evil wanteth a great foil to perceive the beauty of virtue."[35] Spenser himself cited this

principle to justify his recounting of the Malbecco and Hellenore story:

> But never let th'ensample of the bad
> Offend the good: for good, by paragone
> Of evill, may more notably be rad,
> As white seemes fayrer, macht with blacke attone.
>
> (3.9.2)

But ugliness is inherent in Spenser's entire allegorical scheme;
dispraise or blame is as much part of his purpose as praise.
Nevertheless, the artistic value of his images of ugliness may
well merit further scrutiny.

First, the descriptions of ugliness are set pieces, developed
in the classical tradition of *vituperatio* and therefore using the
same topics as encomium. Spenser enumerates the physical
features of Envy just as he did for Belphoebe or Tristram:

> The one of them, that elder did appeare,
> With her dull eyes did seeme to looke askew,
> That her mis-shape much helpt; and her foule heare
> Hung loose and loathsomely: thereto her hew
> Was wan and leane, that all her teeth arew,
> And all her bones might through her cheekes be red:
> Her lips were like raw lether, pale and blew,
> And as she spake, therewith she slavered;
> Yet spake she seldom, but thought more, the lesse she sed.
>
> Her hands were foule and durtie, never washt
> In all her life, with long nayles over raught,
> Like puttocks clawes: with th' one of which she scracht
> Her cursed head, although it itched naught;
> The other held a snake with venime fraught,
> On which she fed and gnawed hungrily,
> As if that long she had not eaten ought;
> That round about her jawes one might descry
> The bloudie gore and poyson dropping lothsomely.
>
> (5.12.29–30)

More emblematic than illusionistic, this portrait emphasizes conventional attributes such as the gnawing on a snake; and even though Envy throws this half-eaten snake at Artegall, she never becomes a figure in the action of the poem, any more than Fidelia, Speranza, and Charissa do.[36] She remains two-dimensional, almost calligraphic, in her features. And here we may be reminded of the place that monstrous images had in Renaissance decorative schemes, with all their implications of variety and humor as they contrast with the beautiful. Indeed, we can see the grotesque unveiling of Duessa as a counterpart to the glorious unveilings of Una's face and hair or Britomart's, both ordinarily concealed by veil or helmet. What Spenser has done is to create a context within which the ugly is as artistically expressive as the beautiful. The decorum of his poem is not violated but rather enhanced by these contrarieties.

Eager as Spenser is to make his readers feel an antipathy to vice, he never loses a sense that he is departing from nature in the exaggeration of repulsive details. But this very lack of realism ensures that ugliness does not disrupt a poem in which everything is stylized according to traditional patterns. The description of Envy is as garnished with appropriate epithets and comparisons as any of the lovely images. In keeping with the rhetorical principle that one should not use inferior comparisons unless "your purpose be to disgrace,"[37] he compares Envy's lips to "raw lether" and her hands to "puttocks clawes." There is a similarly deliberate use of common, low, even obscene words in the description of Duessa's unveiling, because it is Spenser's purpose "to disgrace." For good measure, he adds a conventional apology, that her "secret filth good manners biddeth not to be told." By limiting the attributes of vice figures to the conventional, he contains the reader's emotional response, even to tempering antipathy with humor aroused by details so heightened as to become decorative art rather than the imitation of nature.

But other emotions besides aversion are tempered by the restraints of decorum; for example, the response to both sensuality and suffering. We might find these brought together in uncomfortable fashion in the story of Serena's near miss as a victim to cannibals. But it is significant that the more sensual details of description occur when the cannibals are eyeing the naked woman and that the more modest and tender details occur when Sir Calepine sees his beloved in this wretched state:

> There by th' uncertaine glims of starry night,
> And by the twinkling of their sacred fire,
> He mote perceive a little dawning sight
> Of all which there was doing in that quire:
> Mongst whom a woman spoyld of all attire
> He spyde, lamenting her unluckie strife,
> And groning sore from grieved hart entire;
> Eftsoones he saw one with a naked knife
> Readie to launch her brest, and let out loved life.
>
> (6.8.48)

The moment is dramatically represented with its light-dark contrasts and the naked body opposed to the naked knife so suddenly uplifted. But this shocking and pitiful sight is set under a starry night and the twinkling of the sacred fire: setting and body are both beautiful, and the knife itself seems to gleam out of the darkness. It is difficult to escape the conclusion that decorative considerations are again dominating the depiction and suppressing some of the anguish. Yet the heightening is similar to that in the description of the dying Amavia; in both, it almost reaches the point of sensationalism, only to be turned back by the stylization of the images and their relationship to the moral context. For Spenser, the compatibility of expressiveness with beauty was important,[38] but his task was made the easier by his repertoire of conventional images and his refined sense of the significance that such images can carry. He does not try to make them express anything other than general truths, and whatever care he expends upon their definition is amply repaid by their beauty of form.

All this has a bearing on the difficult question of the Renaissance writer's attitude to his medium. If the clarity of Spenser's images makes everything *seem* nameable, it is still true that the stylization of his depictions means that he confines himself to the universal, to what has already been named, or the available expressive vocabulary.[39] To this extent he operates within the limits of his medium, restrained in his attempts at conveying the inexpressible, keeping instead to the most familiar of circumstances or adjuncts in order to create his illusion. If there is virtuosity, it is the virtuosity of selection and arrangement—verbal patterns devised to reinforce the sense; selection of the most memorable of details stated in the clearest, most compelling words. But selection and arrangement break no new ground in the sense of breaking with tradition; the novelty of Spenser's undertaking lies in his peculiar point of view which shapes his images into uniquely beautiful forms. Paradoxically perhaps, he brings the stock image to definitive perfection through a seriousness of purpose for which all images are only figments or figures. Yet it may be that his use of ready-made schemata allows not only divinity to show itself through the lattice but also the writer himself.[40]

NOTES

1. Puttenham, *Arte,* p. 202.

2. Peacham, *Compleat Gentleman,* p. 84.

3. Northrop Frye, on the other hand, comments in *The Anatomy of Criticism* (Princeton, 1957): "Rhetoric had from the beginning meant two things: ornamented speech and persuasive speech. These two things seem psychologically opposed to each other, as the desire to ornament is essentially disinterested, and the desire to persuade essentially the reverse" (p. 245).

4. See E. H. Gombrich, "Icones Symbolicae," *Symbolic Images* (London, 1972), pp. 123–91.

5. *Ad Herennium,* III.xxii, p. 221. For a fuller discussion of memory theory, see Frances Yates, *The Art of Memory* (London, 1966).

6. Andreas Laurentius, *A Discourse of the Preservation of the Sight,* trans. Richard Surphlet (1599) (London, 1938), p. 75.

7. Abraham Fraunce, *The Lawiers Logike* (1588), p. 41^r.

8. George Richardson, in his *Iconology* (1777), defines iconology as "a species of poetical assistance invented by the ingenious Artist, to give force and expression to the subjects of which he treats" (p. i).

9. *The Rhetoric of Aristotle,* trans. Lane Cooper (New York, 1932), 1411^b, p. 231.

10. Tasso, *Discourses on the Heroic Poem,* p. 74.

11. Sir John Harington, in his trans. of *Orlando Furioso* (1598), VII.46 and XV.95.

12. Sir Francis Bacon, *The Advancement of Learning,* ed. W. A. Wright (Oxford, 1891), p. 208.

13. Thomas Wilson, *The Arte of Rhetorique* (1585), ed. G. H. Mair (Oxford, 1909), pp. 130–31. Cf. Horace, *Ars Poetica,* 102–3: "Si vis me flere, dolendum est / primum ipsi tibi."

14. Dolce, *Aretin,* pp. 163–64. Cf. Roskill, *Dolce's "Aretino,"* p. 157.

15. See Gombrich, *Art and Illusion.*

16. Quintilian, *Institutio Oratoria,* VI.ii.29–36. Cf. Aristotle's *Poetics,* XVII, where the importance for the poet of keeping the scene before his eyes is emphasized.

17. See Hathaway's discussion of Mazzoni in his *Age of Criticism,* pp. 355–84.

18. Erasmus, *On Copia of Words and Ideas,* p. 47. The recent revival of interest in the psychology of visual imagery is reflected, for example, in such a statement as the following: "Surely much of the craft of the creative writer consists in his ability to transfer to the mind of his reader the images he has constructed within his own mind" (Cohen, "Visual Imagery in Thought," p. 517).

19. Philostratus, *Life of Apollonius,* trans. F. C. Conybeare (London, 1912), 1:177.

20. Leonardo da Vinci, *Treatise on Painting,* 1:156.

21. Lomazzo, *A Tracte Containing the Artes,* trans. Richard Haydocke (Oxford, 1958), p. 10.

22. Peacham, *Garden of Eloquence* (1593), p. 146.

23. On formulaic language in epic poetry, see C. M. Bowra, *Heroic Poetry* (London, 1952), pp. 215–53. C. S. Lewis's failure to note the oral nature of Spenser's style led to his disparaging remarks about "Spenser's eulogistic or dyslogistic adjectives" (*Allegory of Love,* p. 319).

24. See Rudolf Arnheim, *Art and Visual Perception* (Berkeley, 1964), p. 368.

25. The ironic verbal echoes of "faire" in relationship to the word "farr" of the preceding line are noted in Martha Craig's essay "The Secret Wit of Spenser's Language," in *Elizabethan Poetry,* ed. Paul J. Alpers (New York, 1967), p. 454.

26. Longinus, *On the Sublime,* trans. W. Hamilton Fyfe, Loeb Classical Library, rev. ed. (1932; rpt. Cambridge, Mass., 1965), p. 205. Cf. W. Rhys Roberts's trans. (Cambridge, 1899), XXVIII.1, p. 115.

27. Faral, *Les Arts Poétiques,* p. 76.

28. On the differences between Mercilla and Lucifera, see Cain, *Praise in the Faerie Queene,* p. 41.

29. Tasso, *Discourses on the Heroic Poem,* p. 135.

30. Balthasar Gracián, *Art of Worldly Wisdom* (1653), cxxvii, trans. Joseph Jacobs (London, 1892), p. 74.

31. George Herbert, *A Priest to the Temple, or, The Country Parson,* in *Works,* ed. F. E. Hutchinson (Oxford, 1941), p. 233. Cited in Annabel M. Patterson, *Hermogenes and the Renaissance: Seven Ideas of Style* (Princeton, 1970), p. 22.

32. See Puttenham, *Arte,* for example, III.xxiii. I have not attempted to take up Annabel Patterson's challenge to explore fully the decorum of Spenser's poem, because that would be another, different book. See Patterson, *Hermogenes and the Renaissance,* pp. 211–12. Rosemond Tuve comments on the difficulty of the task: "As his tone constantly shifts in accordance with decorum, a matter handled with extreme artistry, and one we are barely well enough educated to apprehend, we see the influence of something much more considered than a vague serene idealism" (*Allegorical Imagery,* p. 387).

33. Tasso, *Discourses on the Heroic Poem,* p. 92. Cf. Cicero, *De Officiis,* 1.27.

34. Puttenham, *Arte,* p. 149.

35. Sidney, *Apology for Poetry,* p. 117.

36. On the emblematic tradition for Spenser's Envy, see Jack W. Jessee, "Spenser and the Emblem Book" (Diss., Univ. of Kentucky, 1955), pp. 131–32.

37. John Hoskins, *Directions for Speech and Style,* p. 9.

38. Lessing, of course, thought that the compatibility of expressiveness with beauty was the concern of the plastic arts and not of literature. See *Laocoon,* ch. 2, for example.

39. E. H. Gombrich discusses "the available expressive vocabulary" in many of his works, including several of the essays in *Meditations on a Hobby Horse.*

40. Cf. Sir Thomas Browne on how divinity shows itself through the lattice of the temple ("The Garden of Cyrus," in

The Prose of Sir Thomas Browne, ed. N. Endicott [Garden City, 1967], p. 303). Cf. also Curtius on how literary forms have the function of lattices (*European Literature and the Latin Middle Ages,* p. 390). See p. 88.

CHAPTER 6

The Poet as Painter

I

There is no more interesting or crucial question about Spenser's imagery than how his use of stylized patterns turns into illusionistic fiction. How do spider and bee become reconciled in his work? The last three chapters have been chiefly concerned with the work of the bee: the conventional forms which constitute the language of the poem and the way these lend themselves to decorative and expressive effect. There remains the question of how the poet uses this language to paint pictures for his audience—that is, to transcend the limits of the verbal medium and make the readers see what he describes. Only the words will tell us what we are to see, but, in part, whether we see anything at all depends upon our own receptivity to the words of the poem.

"Making images with the mind alone" may be a creative act, but it is language that gives the vision visible form, blocks it off and shapes it in a way analogous to the painter's; words can be very definite about the pictorial quality of an experience, however vague they may be about some of the details. Spenser must have known precisely what pictures he wanted to convey. Not only is his fantasy world immediately recognizable, as in a fairy tale, but the way each image is shaped for beauty and expressiveness transforms the familiar into the extraordinary; so faithfully does he adhere to the fantasy image by his acceptance of tradition, finding the right words by remaining true to the language of medieval romance, that his energy can then be devoted to shaping this image as a pictorial work of art.

This is not ordinarily the kind of image found in narrative poetry. Whether we consider Shakespeare's or Marlowe's narrative poems, or Ariosto's and Tasso's, despite all their differences in style and point of view, we find that the most vivid imagery is still subordinated to narrative flow in a way Spenser does not intend. I say "intend" on the assumption that he knew what he was doing in making his images self-contained entities. Yet it must be maintained that this was not a purely artistic (or intellectual, for that matter) deci-sion—otherwise it could not so communicate itself to the reader—but the natural outcome of the way his imagination worked.

In considering the problem of analyzing the visual experi-ence provided by the poem, one need not evade the assump-tion that Spenser first had the experience he describes: as noted in the last chapter, both ancient and Renaissance critics lend support to this view. A Renaissance rhetorician tells us, for example, that "Sir Philip Sidney's course was . . . to imagine the thing present in his own brain that his pen might the better present it to you."[1] But in general, Renaissance writers do not explain in any detail how this happens. We can probably learn more about the workings of the imagination from ancient writers, such as Philostratus in his account of Apollonius of Tyana. Here we are told that "imagination . . . is a wiser and subtler artist by far than imitation: for imitation can only create as its handiwork what it has seen, but imagi-nation equally what it has not seen."[2] In a discussion of painting, this same sage refers to the clouds and what can be seen in them—centaurs, stag-antelopes, wolves, or horses. They "flit through heaven," he says, "not only without meaning, but so far as providence is concerned, by mere chance; while we who by nature are prone to imitation rearrange and create them in these regular figures."[3] The discussion that follows contains some interesting observations on the art of painting, but unfortunately nothing on imitation by means of words. Yet we may perhaps see an analogy between the fantasy images of the mind, or the cloud images, and how these become "rearranged and turned into regular figures" by an art of words that has to be acquired, just as the art of representational drawing has to be acquired. The difference is that the words, unlike the drawing or painting, require that the image appear in the mind alone; the words, then, can only mediate between the image in the mind of the poet and the image in the mind of the reader.

Spenser's image in words is nicely calculated to produce exactly the image in the reader's mind which was already there and only waiting to be called into activity. When it is so called, it has all the charm of fresh experience, however, having acquired a music, a rhythm, *and* a definition that were not there before. It has, as well, its form enhanced, or strengthened, by possessing a new significance. What had been merely idle fantasy is now high art, something to be experienced, something tangible, existing in the form of words no less certainly than an image exists in the form of paint.

The experience of satisfying form sets off the poetic image from the fantasy image as surely as art is set off from dream. But, as Apollonius points out, in recognizing a pictorial image one must have the idea of the thing, whether a horse or anything else, already in one's mind in order to recognize the painted depiction. What he says of those who look at works

of painting and drawing, that they "require a mimetic faculty," applies also to the reading of poetry. If the reader lacks
the mimetic faculty, he cannot receive the images intended
by the poet, no matter how well he reads. Apollonius exemplifies: "for no one could appreciate or admire a picture of a
horse or of a bull, unless he had formed an idea of the creature represented. Nor again could one admire a picture of
Ajax, by the painter Timomachus, which represents him in a
state of madness, unless one had conceived in one's mind first
an idea or notion of Ajax, and had entertained the probability
that after killing the flocks in Troy he would sit down ex-
hausted and meditate suicide."[4] Just such a range of imaginative comprehension must be postulated for a reader if he is to
receive the images Spenser provides. It is no use turning to
the color-blind for an interpretation of the works of Titian.

At the same time, the models suggested for visual perception do not altogether supply a means of understanding the
poetic image, any more than actual paintings do. Both kinds
of analogizing impose a literalism upon what is essentially
fluid and subject, not to the laws of matter, but to the laws of
an inner perception in accordance with one's deepest sympathies and antipathies. The poet is limited neither by his
bodily sight nor by the need to depict a three-dimensional
image on a two-dimensional surface. In his *Icones,* Lucian refers to Homer as "best of painters," surpassing even Apelles,
and he concludes his portrait of the ideal woman by saying
that such a work, if perfectly executed, "will be far removed
from creations of wood and wax and colour, being inspired
by the Muses, in whom alone is that true portraiture that
shows forth in one likeness a lovely body and a virtuous
soul."[5] Renaissance critics repeated this argument in favor of
the superiority of poets over painters, especially when they
were defending narrative poetry as imitation. Thus Mazzoni

remarks that "the image in the poetic narrative surpasses in distinctness and clarity that of a picture itself."[6] This use of the *paragone* does, I think, remind us of an essential aspect of the poet's freedom: painting not for the outer eye but for the inner, he is not dependent upon line and color for his image but may depict whatever he has seen in his mind and can find words for.

In his capacity to visualize everything he describes, Spenser seems to fit Junius's account of Ovid:

> When Ovid doth describe that same temerary ladde that foolishly longed to tread upon his Fathers fiery chariot, would you not thinke then that the Poet stepping with *Phaeton* upon the waggon hath noted from the beginning to the end every particular accident which could fall out in such a horrible confusion? Neither could he ever have conceived the least shadow of this dangerous enterprise, if he had not been as if it were present with the unfortunate youth: he beholdeth first the impatient horses standing as yet within the barres, how by treading and trampling they do spend before the race thousand and thousand steppes to no purpose: afterwards doth he see the vaine stripling skip upon the waggon, and with a brave undaunted looke drive on, till the fierce winged beasts perceiving the impotency of their new Master throw the unexperienced waggoner headlong downe with waggon and all.[7]

At this point Junius directs the reader to turn to Ovid himself and other poets if he would understand "what vehement and sensible Imaginations they have followed; and that without such a force of phantasie the whole labour of their braines will be but a heavie, dull, and lifeless piece of worke."[8] It is this capacity in Spenser that seems to give us an eyewitness account of everything that happens in *The Faerie Queene.* He

can tell us exactly the appearance of anyone or anything, so
that whether his descriptions are general or detailed, they
imply that his knowledge is complete.

While recognizing Spenser's debt to pictorial convention,
we have therefore to guard against limiting his powers of imagery to the representation of actual works of art.[9] In effect,
the poet can portray what the painter strives to attain:

> Beside his head there satt a faire young man,
> Of wondrous beauty and of freshest yeares,
> Whose tender bud to blossome new began,
> And florish faire above his equall peares:
> His snowy front, curled with golden heares,
> Like Phoebus face adorned with sunny rayes,
> Divinely shone, and two sharpe winged sheares,
> Decked with diverse plumes, like painted jayes,
> Were fixed at his backe, to cut his ayery wayes.
>
> (2.8.5)

There is an airiness in this image that even one of Fra An-
gelico's beautiful angels does not possess—a kind of divinity,
too, beside which painted angels are likely to seem merely
charming. The features may closely resemble the depiction
of angels and Cupid in manuscript illuminations, but when
Spenser describes his angel's youth and beauty, he can make
the image shine more brightly than gold paint can do, because the gold paint has certain physical limitations, like all
the other colors a painter may use. Free from these limitations, Spenser is able to make us see colors which he does
not even name: "Decked with diverse plumes, like painted
jayes." To expand the range of his image, he has a stanza-long
simile comparing this angel to Cupid in his benevolent and
joyous mood. For the poet, there is a rapture in such allusions to the world of classical mythology, but he returns with
a more solemn voice to the palmer's view of the angel at
Guyon's head:

Whom when the palmer saw, abasht he was
Through fear and wonder, that he nought could say.

(2.8.7)

The contrast with the frivolity of Cupid is clear, yet the image of divine love remains as a mystery enhanced by this allusion. The vanishing of the angel after he speaks is as marvellous as his appearance, and we gaze after him along with the palmer:

So having said, eftsoones he gan display
His painted nimble wings, and vanisht quite away.

The palmer seeing his lefte empty place,
And his slow eies beguiled of their sight,
Woxe sore affraid, and standing still a space,
Gaz'd after him, as fowle escapt by flight.

(2.8.8–9)

Now we note another advantage of the poet, that he is able to show the angel not only sitting on earth but flying away; those gorgeous wings will actually carry him, whereas they are more strictly an attribute for most painters, although the greatest will be able to suggest flight even in their motionless angels. The difference between the poet and painter is, then, not one of purpose but of means. The difficulty for the poet is to make us see the image palpably; the difficulty for the painter is to give it the breath of life and motion. If we remember that any of the art Spenser might have seen would fall far short of his own pictorial imagination, we may be more likely to do him the justice of recognizing that his images cannot entirely be accounted for by any precedent in the visual arts.

II

What faithfulness to the inner vision requires of the poet is above all a language that will reflect without distortion. Not wishing to draw the reader's attention to the words so much as to the image, Spenser is content with stock expressions as the most unobtrusive clues to a familiar realm of the imagination. For this purpose, too, a storyteller of a certain cast of mind is needed, one whose simplicity of character allows him to wonder and marvel at the show passing through his mind's eye; one who also believes in the power of words to conjure up pictures. These characteristics belong to the decorum of the poet as old-fashioned storyteller; yet insofar as he is an artist, he cannot be content with mere story but must shape the image in the interests of beauty. Here we have the whole paradox of Spenser's language: that it should be at once so simple and pure, and at the same time, so subtle and ornamental in form. The poet is the one who must hold these two aspects in his hand, almost as Apollo holds the Graces in his.

In the poem, we seem to hear two voices: one in the proems to the separate books; the other, the voice which recounts the tales. It would be easy to assume that Spenser speaks in his own person in the proems because there he defends and explains his purpose, whereas in the narrative proper a persona of the poet appears to be speaking. Indeed Spenser almost seems to justify such an interpretation in the very first lines of the poem:

Lo! I the man, whose Muse whylome did maske,
As time her taught, in lowly shephards weeds,
Am now enforst a far unfitter taske,
For trumpets sterne to chaunge mine oaten reeds,
And sing of knights and ladies gentle deeds;
Whose praises having slept in silence long,
Me, all too meane, the sacred Muse areeds
To blazon broade emongst her learned throng:
Fierce warres and faithfull loves shall moralize my song.
                                                            (1.Proem.1)

Sidney also refers in his *Apology* to "the masquing raiment of poesy," which is similar to Spenser's masking "in lowly shephards weeds." This metaphor, as well as the musical one by which the poet shifts from "oaten reeds" to "trumpets sterne," suggests that he must adopt a form of expression, a genre, and all that goes with it. But our modern concept of persona does not quite fit the Renaissance poet's attitude simply because it assumes that a poet may speak in his own person. Of course Renaissance critics allow for this as a possibility, but they do so in terms that suggest a certain artifice in obedience to the claims of decorum, and hence nothing resembling the self-expression of a romantic or modern poet. When they think of a poet as speaking in his own person in a lyric or sometimes in an epic, it is the poet as the poet of a particular genre; for example the poet of epic will be wearing his singing robes and be crowned with the bays. In this opening stanza, then, Spenser distinguishes between himself and the voice speaking in his poem and, at the same time, makes even the allusion to himself so conventional as to show that he is adopting the traditional role of epic poet. He is showing his awareness of the stylistic requirements of the different genres, as he tries to win the goodwill of the audience.

His use of the humility topos is another of the ways by which to win this goodwill: "me, all too meane." But similar conventions govern the narrator's references to himself in the body of the poem. He too is a poet, lamenting that his "ragged rimes are all too rude and bace" (1.12.13); he too feels the weariness of composing a long tale (cf. 1.12.44 with 6.Proem.1). They are in fact the same person with the same sensibilities and values. What differences there are may be briefly comprehended under the general distinction between Spenser as the poet of the whole and Spenser the storyteller. The latter of necessity does not discuss his choice of meta-

phors as the poet of the proems does; he cannot be allowed
to speak as the inventor of the fiction because he must speak
as the historian of what has happened.

First, he names things as if the mere assertion that they
exist were enough to persuade the reader that they do. This
seemingly naive attitude to language already puts us in a receptive frame of mind, for we read "A gentle knight was
pricking on the plaine" as an invitation to an enchanted land.
The words stand for concepts—yes, but in a sense unknown
to us, they *are* the concepts, so that to name is to summon the
things named: "he by wordes could call out of the sky / Both
sunne and moone" (3.3.12).

The storyteller's faith in his own vision reveals itself in
every line. For example, the syntax of the narrative is primarily concerned with telling us the position of things in relationship to the setting and to one another or to sequence of
events, so that the connection of ideas is fairly simple. Since
most lines are end-stopped, the effect is additive, and each
thing stands out in its own particular identity. A stanza chosen at random will serve to illustrate Spenser's use of this
"natural" language of medieval romance:[10]

> But Tristram, then despoyling that dead knight
> Of all those goodly implements of prayse,
> Long fed his greedie eyes with the faire sight
> Of the bright mettall, shyning like sunne rayes;
> Handling and turning them a thousand wayes.
> And, after having them upon him dight,
> He tooke that ladie, and her up did rayse
> Upon the steed of her owne late dead knight,
> So with her marched forth, as she did him behight.
>
> (6.2.39)

This loose, casual, additive style, with its easy rhythm and
predominantly colloquial vocabulary, implies that the story-

teller is not imposing his interpretation upon a world so much as recording what he sees in the fashion of a chronicler.

Most often we are shown what someone in the poem is actually witnessing, ensuring that descriptions grow out of the action and lead into it. Consider, for example, how Artegall comes upon a crowd of warlike women:

> And in the midst of them he saw a knight,
> With both his hands behinde him pinnoed hard,
> And round about his necke an halter tight,
> As ready for the gallow tree prepared:
> His face was covered, and his head was bar'd,
> That who he was uneath was to descry.
>
> (5.4.22)

The point of view of the spectator is preserved by the gradual giving of information, as he moves closer to the scene. It is not that Spenser is interested in the painter's use of perspective but that he tries to make us as readers share the visual experience of the character whose adventures he is following at that particular moment.[11] But since the poet sees everything, too, he can, when he chooses, give his own description, without restricting himself to the point of view of one of the characters. The portrait of Belphoebe departs from what Trompart could see. Not only does it include such elaborate details as the fastenings of her buskins but also praise for her chastity; there is even a reference to her "Sweete wordes, like dropping honny" before she has uttered a word. Spenser does not hesitate to make identifications which the spectator in the story could not possibly make but which are necessary to the completeness of the image. So too, in describing the golden apples of the Garden of Proserpina in Book II, he goes beyond their appearance to enrich their meaning by allusions to all the golden apples of classical mythology. Where an image has this kind of far-reaching significance, Spenser is quite ready to go beyond the visual aspects.

Nevertheless, his constant references to verbs and nouns of sight point to the fact that experience within the poem is primarily visual.[12] Indeed, so absorbed are the characters in the visual that adjectives suggest a kind of lust of the eye: Britomart gazes with "greedy eyes" at the marvels of the House of Busirane; Sir Scudamore views the Temple of Venus with "gazefull eye"; Tristram feeds "his greedie eyes" with the sight of the weapons he has taken from a vanquished opponent; Calidore envies his own eyes the joy of seeing the Graces dance. All these characters share the same intensity of visual experience that Spenser as storyteller exhibits. He seizes upon certain distinctive physical features in the people he describes: their hair (matted or rayed out or flowing), their hands (large, lily-white, or clawlike), their eyes (glaring, greedy, or fair). Like attributes, these are clues to character and reinforce the significance of actual attributes, such as the club of Disdain or the arrows of Belphoebe. Dress is another distinguishing characteristic: the ragged garment of Despair expresses his character, just as the attire of an Amazon expresses hers. Of course none of these are merely identifying features, but rather each of them evokes either sympathy or antipathy in the spectator and is chosen for this reason. Seeing and feeling are so much one and the same that the didactic message of emblem is experienced firsthand, through the language of pleasure and pain, without the interposition of sophisticated judgment.

The figure of Disdain in Book VI, for example, takes on a nightmare quality from the strongly marked features singled out as if they were seen from the child's point of view: height, eyes, scornful expression, Moorish attire, black hair, and, finally, club.

For he was sterne and terrible by nature,
And eeke of person huge and hideous,
Exceeding much the measure of mans stature,
And rather like a gyant monstruous. . . .

His lookes were dreadfull, and his fiery eies,
Like two great beacons, glared bright and wyde,
Glauncing askew, as if his enemies
He scorned in his overweening pryde;
And stalking stately like a crane, did stryde
At every step uppon the tiptoes hie;
And all the way he went, on every syde
He gaz'd about, and stared horriblie,
As if he with his lookes would all men terrifie.

He wore no armour, ne for none did care,
As no whit dreading any living wight;
But in a jacket, quilted richly rare
Upon checklaton, he was straungely dight;
And on his head a roll of linnen plight,
Like to the Mores of Malaber, he wore,
With which his locks, as blacke as pitchy night,
Were bound about, and voyded from before;
And in his hand a mighty yron club he bore.

(6.7.41–43)

The adjectives and adverbs—"sterne and terrible," "dread-full," "horriblie"—underline the viewer's response to this alien and threatening being. The illusion of seeing depends, however, less upon the assemblage of traditional attributes, such as those of Daunger in medieval romance, than upon the mental image which Spenser seems to have before him as he writes and to which he responds;[13] this response alone gives coherence to the enumeration of features. Similes, like the rest of the diction, help to establish the affective tone, conventional though they are: eyes "like two great beacons," stalking "like a crane," locks "as blacke as pitchy night." The visible becomes one with the emotional in a way that emblematic depiction could not accomplish, lacking as it does a narrative context.

Other visually arresting features that attract the storyteller's attention are color and light contrasts. He notes the white and the black of Una's robe or red blood on green grass; he likes, perhaps most of all, the glitter of gold, whether sprinkled on ivory or in the form of golden hair, adorning the "snowy front" of an angel. But even colorlessness, if extreme, will catch his eye:

> As pale and wan as ashes was his looke,
> His body leane and meagre as a rake,
> And skin all withered like a dryed rooke,
> Thereto as cold and drery as a snake,
> That seemd to tremble evermore, and quake;
> All in a canvas thin he was bedight,
> And girded with a belt of twisted brake:
> Upon his head he wore an helmet light,
> Made of a dead mans skull, that seemd a ghastly sight.
>   (2.11.22)

Apart from the paleness of his face, Maleger's garment lacks any color, as does his strange helmet, the striking detail on which Spenser, as so often, chooses to conclude his stanza. As color is associated with life in Spenser's images, so its absence in this image suggests a terrifying morbidity.

Contrasts of light and darkness also have their affective and hence symbolic overtones, and, like the color contrasts, they lend themselves to dramatic visual effects, especially in caves. When Red Cross looked into Error's den, he was looking into a "darksom hole" where "his glistring armor made / A litle glooming light, much like a shade, / By which he saw the ugly monster plaine" (1.1.14). Transparent though the moral symbolism may be, the image has a pictorial interest derived from

the very ambiguity of a light which is "much like a shade." It
is perhaps an attempt to define in words what can be more
easily represented in paint, but more than once Spenser tried
to put this effect into words. He does it in the Cave of Mammon in a more mysterious way, with the help of two similes:

> for vew of cherefull day
> Did never in that house it selfe display,
> But a faint shadow of uncertein light;
> Such as a lamp, whose life does fade away;
> Or as the moone, cloathed with clowdy night,
> Does shew to him that walkes in feare and sad affright.
>
> (2.7.29)

He does it again in describing the cave of thieves, where
Pastorella was taken:

> But darkenesse dred and daily night did hover
> Through all the inner parts, wherein they dwelt;
> Ne lightned was with window nor with lover,
> But with continuall candlelight, which delt
> A doubtfull sense of things, not so well seene as felt.
>
> (6.10.42)

What light there is in this evil place is artificial, not natural.
Pastorella herself creates a light that is sharply distinguished
from the light cast by the candles:

> The sight of whom, though now decayd and mard,
> And eke but hardly seene by candle-light,
> Yet like a diamond of rich regard,
> In doubtfull shadow of the darkesome night,
> With starrie beames about her shining bright,
> These marchants fixed eyes did so amaze.
>
> (6.11.13)

As everywhere in the poem, the visual is perceived as both an
affective experience and a moral one inviting judgment. Indeed, a purely aesthetic point of view would diminish the

reality of such scenes, which owe their vitality chiefly to the storyteller's vivid participation in the events he describes.

Yet there is one visual feature frequently noted in the poem that suggests less of emotional impact and more of artistic interest. I refer to the ornamental aspect of the images, discussed in Chapter 4. Undoubtedly, such a detached appreciation of decorative features has a suggestion of Homer's descriptive style, as in the description of how Arthur's sword is hung

> In yvory sheath, ycarv'd with curious slights;
> Whose hilts were burnisht gold, and handle strong
> Of mother perle, and buckled with a golden tong.
> (1.7.30)

But it is not simply that Spenser is following epic tradition in magnifying the importance of the hero's weapon in this way; there is a true, if almost primitive, pleasure in the richness and the intricacy of workmanship. We are perhaps reminded of the ornamental surface of an early Renaissance portrait, with its careful embroidery, its sharply defined lace. Instead of depicting only the actual surface appearances of things, these artists were resolved upon making every detail completely visible, just as Spenser the storyteller is intent upon the objective details of things as if they were seen in one constant, clear illumination. He is totally absorbed in whatever feature he is gazing at. If such immersion in the moment of seeing, with its innocent admiration, gives him his spellbinding power of description, it also suggests something of the butterfly in *Muiopotmos* who tastes of every flower. Yet coming to grips with evil, as he must, commits him to judgment.

In handing over his fiction to a narrator who is in some ways distinguishable from the poet, Spenser invents a storyteller who is both "medium" and partial interpreter, but the larger part he plays is as "medium." It would not do for him to be able to interpret everything, for that would be to lose the richness of the metaphor which the poet has been at such pains to preserve in his explanatory proems. More accurately, the pretense of oral narration conveys a sense of the withheld, rather than ignorant, interpretation, which has the effect of engaging the reader in active assessment.

It is also clear that Spenser is trying to gain the advantages of innocence for the assessment of the corruption to be found in this world. Even the narrator's professed admiration for the "goodly workmanship" of the Bower of Bliss is innocent, although the Bower is not. In lamenting its destruction—"of the fayrest late, now made the fowlest place"—he is only preserving the consistency of his own attitude toward beauty of craftsmanship. But now innocence becomes tinged with irony, so that the effect is of a dual perspective on the sensuous experience: the one, the response of sensual man; the other, the response of enlightened man, who sees beyond appearances. In this way, the morality of art, or the relationship between the beautiful and the good, can be explored, not doctrinally but experientially.

These ironic praises of "forged" beauty entirely derive their significance from the character of the narrator: given his love of beauty and his simplicity, it might seem that he could be taken in by appearances, but his deeper knowledge gives him the ability—however concealed—to discriminate between the false and the true. He is not a Gulliver or, for that matter, a medieval poet, such as Chaucer, who makes full ironic use of the ignorant pose. Rather, it is as if he combined the roles of Dante and Virgil in *The Divine Comedy,* so that he can respond with wonder to all that he sees and yet be aware of its limits as a manifestation of truth.[14]

This narrator is not, of course, a personality in the sense that Dante is in his epic, but then he is not an actor in his tale

and goes on no journey himself. As the anonymous storyteller of medieval romance, it is only necessary for him to suit
his tone to the time and place of his story. That these are in
the past age of chivalry, a more heroic time than the present,
requires a respect or veneration for the values that are represented; that the events are marvellous requires also the innocence of childhood. Both constitute that ethos or character
which, as Aristotle said, is almost "the most potent of all the
means to persuasion."[15] Consider, for example, that the expressiveness of the imagery depends upon the conviction
with which the speaker tells us what constitutes an occasion
for wonder, sympathy, or antipathy. It is not enough for him
to say: "So oft as I this history record, / My heart doth melt
with mere compassion" (3.8.1). He must also portray with
tenderness the dying Amavia and with delicacy the feelings of
Serena when she is about to be sacrificed. It is his consistency
of moral judgment that is our best assurance that he can be
trusted. Thus he is fully aware, according to his lights, both of
the heavenly origins of compassion ("And is there care in
heaven?") and of the need for "rigor pitilesse" against the
forces of darkness. If conventional moralizing is to ring true,
the character of the narrator must lend it weight.

    In brief, his character allows formulas to spring to life.
Certainly illusion would be impossible if this could not hap-
pen. Like singing a familiar tune, the well-worn notes of such
expressions as "so faire and fresh as freshest flowre in May"
(1.12.22) generate their own feeling—at least for those who
respond to the repetition. Evidently the narrator is one who
does and who is therefore able to beguile us into sharing his
experience. Once we fall under his spell, we become receptive to whatever he chooses to tell us, whether it is illusionistic in the sense of possessing dramatic reality, whether it is a
static emblem, like Faith, Hope, and Charity, or whether it is

commentary on the action. Everything depends upon the relationship established between reader and narrator.[16]

Indeed, the childlike values of romance easily join hands with the moral values that Spenser wishes to teach. But if the naive style is really a sophisticated mask, is the innocent point of view also? After all, the poet knows the deceptiveness of appearances, would not value the Bower of Bliss, and yet has his narrator seem to. But although the narrator is apparently less omniscient than the poet—witness his many references to "fortune or grace" as alternative explanations for what happens—nevertheless they have, as one would expect, a powerful affinity in their values. Spenser, for example, always had a taste for the beauty and the apparent naiveté of the archaic, as can be seen in *The Shepheardes Calender* and *Colin Clouts Come Home Againe.* His use of archaic diction accords well with Demetrius's statement that "an old-fashioned style" betokens an innocent nature, "the ancients being distinguished by naiveté."[17] For Spenser, it seems safe to say that his masks of naiveté and innocence were at least in part representations of his own self, although shaped to the rhetorical needs of his poems.

III

No doubt some of the visual intensity of the image in *The Faerie Queene* derives from the innocence of the storyteller, as well as from the tendency of romance to provide spectacle, or a succession of wonders, for the eye. What he shows us is what he himself has seen; in the words of Longinus, "the image in his mind he almost compelled his audience to behold."[18] But the other part is due to the particular ordering of the images as pictures. So careful is this patterning that it almost runs counter to the onward narrative movement. This can most readily be seen if we compare his descriptions with those of Chaucer. A battle description has the disadvantage of showing Spenser at his most formulaic, but, for that very reason, it may help to indicate some of his artistic concerns. First, Chaucer's description of a battle in *The Knight's Tale:*

> Now ryngen trompes loude and clarioun.
> Ther is namoore to seyn, but west and est
> In goon the speres ful sadly in arrest;
> In gooth the sharpe spore into the syde.
> Ther seen men who kan juste and who kan ryde;
> Ther shyveren shaftes upon sheeldes thikke;
> He feeleth thurgh the herte-spoon the prikke.
> Up spryngen speres twenty foot on highte;
> Out goon the swerdes as the silver brighte;
> The helmes they tohewen and toshrede;
> Out brest the blood with stierne stremes rede;
> With myghty maces the bones they tobreste.
>
> (KT2600–2611)

Beside this description, Spenser's battles seem lifeless, as if the formulas failed to inspire him; yet the disorder of combat takes on in his hands a definition that possesses decorative appeal.

> A shrilling trompett sownded from on hye,
> And unto battaill bad them selves addresse:
> Their shining shieldes about their wrestes they tye,
> And burning blades about their heads doe blesse,
> The instruments of wrath and heavinesse:
> With greedy force each other doth assayle,
> And strike so fiercely, that they doe impresse
> Deepe dinted furrowes in the battred mayle:
> The yron walles to ward their blowes are weak and fraile.
>
> (1.5.6)

Instead of aiming at an effect of tumult, Spenser carefully divides his action into phases, so that he can fit each to the divisions of his stanza: the first quatrain is bright with sound and glittering weapons as the battle is launched; the second turns to the effect of these "instruments of wrath and heavinesse" upon the combatants' armor; the alexandrine reflects on the weakness of the "yron walles" to withstand such blows. So leisurely and orderly is Spenser's stage-by-stage account that it takes him almost another three stanzas to arrive at the inevitable "streames of blood." The formulas are the same as Chaucer's but Spenser's instinct for stylized pattern is so great that he seems to make ballets out of the traditional chivalric battles.

As another example of the way he selects and arranges details to fit his stanza form, as compared with the more casual and indiscriminate piling up of details in Chaucer's *Knight's Tale,* we may compare Spenser's description of Radigund with Chaucer's description of Emetreus, King of India:

> Upon a steede bay trapped in steel,
> Covered in clooth of gold, dyapred weel,
> Cam ridynge lyk the god of armes, Mars.
> His cote-armure was of clooth of Tars
> Couched with perles white and rounde and grete;
> His sadel was of brend gold newe ybete;
> A mantelet upon his shulder hangynge,
> Bret-ful of rubyes rede as fyr sparklynge;
> His crispe heer lyk rynges was yronne,
> And that was yelow, and glytered as the sonne.
> His nose was heigh, his eyen bright citryn,
> His lippes rounde, his colour was sangwyn;
> A fewe frakenes in his face yspreynd,
> Bitwixen yelow and somdel blak ymeynd;
> And as a leon he his lookyng caste.
>
> (KT2157–71)

This description continues for another ten lines, but it is unnecessary to quote further to make the point that this style of description would never satisfy Spenser's artistic sensibility. It is not the number of lines used, or even the enumerative method, that distinguishes Spenser from Chaucer, but the selection and arrangement of details. If we now examine Spenser's portrait of Radigund, we can see not only how Spenser puts artistic selection above a mantle "bret-ful of rubyes" but also how he composes his picture in relation to the stanza frame:

> All in a camis light of purple silke
> Woven uppon with silver, subtly wrought,
> And quilted uppon sattin white as milke,
> Trayled with ribbands diversly distraught,
> Like as the workeman had their courses taught;
> Which was short tucked for light motion
> Up to her ham, but, when she list, it raught
> Downe to her lowest heele, and thereuppon
> She wore for her defence a mayled habergeon.
>
> And on her legs she painted buskins wore,
> Basted with bends of gold on every side,
> And mailes betweene, and laced close afore:
> Uppon her thigh her cemitare was tide,
> With an embrodered belt of mickell pride;
> And on her shoulder hung her shield, bedeckt
> Uppon the bosse with stones, that shined wide
> As the faire moone in her most full aspect,
> That to the moone it mote be like in each respect.
>
> (5.5.2-3)

Both stanzas dwell upon the fine workmanship of her attire, but the first is concerned with her chief garments and the second with her armaments and smaller gear, ending with the dramatic image of the moonlike shield, which seems to sum up her own splendor. There is none of the random collection of details that we may see in Chaucer's description. At the same time, this selection and arrangement within the stanza frame suggests a pictorial conception that seems to transcend the enumerative method.

This art of pictorial composition Spenser may have learned in part from Ariosto, but also he could have learned it from Renaissance aesthetic values in general: what was left out could be as important as what was put into the picture. The temptations of descriptive *varietas,* willingly acceded to by Chaucer, were now to be kept in check by larger humanist concerns, such as the dignity, harmony, and unity of the composition.[19] But temperament—dare one use the word?— gives to these spacious pictures an air of motionlessness, an objectivity suggesting the unmoving eye of God. Someone is seeing and seeing with a visionary intensity which cannot but modify the way we as readers respond both to the visual patterning and to the narrative flow. What might have been elegant embroidery, on the one hand, or enthralling story, on the other hand, turns out to have characteristics of both, but, as well, a contemplative spirit which may have affinities with the emblem tradition but is wholly Spenser's own.

The mode of seeing in the poem patterns everything, including the conspicuously ugly. In Chapter 4, this interest in the ornateness of the individual image was considered but it must now be viewed in the wider context of narrative and allegory. If every moment of the poem is intended to be beautiful, regardless of subject matter, this interest will to some extent run counter to the onward movement of the story. Throughout the poem, there seems almost a denial of time, from the gentle knight pricking on an endless plain, through the static battles in which the figures assume heraldic poses, to the Graces dancing in their timeless world. Florimell in her headlong flight becomes immovable on seeing a fisherman asleep in his boat with the nets drying on the sand:

It fortuned (High God did so ordaine)
As shee arrived on the roring shore,
In mind to leape into the mighty maine,
A little bote lay hoving her before,
In which there slept a fisher old and pore,
The whiles his nets were drying on the sand:
Into the same shee lept, and with the ore
Did thrust the shallop from the floting strand:
So safety fownd at sea, which she fownd not at land.

(3.7.27)

The scene is shown as Florimell saw it, and yet so vivid is
the three-line sketch of this sea idyll that for a moment all
thought of her dire need vanishes as the scene is contemplated.

A little bote lay hoving her before,
In which there slept a fisher old and pore,
The whiles his nets were drying on the sand.

But this pause to contemplate the scene is only for an instant;
before the stanza ends, the action has resumed and the motionless picture has changed. Spenser's imagery exhibits this
constant fluctuation between contemplation and action. Yet
so perfect is the contemplation while it lasts that the image
seems utterly timeless; so complete is the spectator's absorp-
tion that momentarily the action seems suspended. Then like
magic the picture quickens into life.

But the picture sometimes remains motionless to the end
of the stanza, as in the following scene which we view
through Britomart's eyes:

At last, as nigh out of the wood she came,
A stately castle far away she spyde,
To which her steps directly she did frame.
That castle was most goodly edifyde,
And plaste for pleasure nigh that forrest syde:

But faire before the gate a spatious playne,
Mantled with greene, it self did spredden wyde,
On which she saw six knights, that did darrayne
Fiers battaill against one, with cruel might and mayne.

(3.1.20)

One could not improve upon this as a fine example of the
formulaic style which nevertheless attains illusion through a
sureness of touch by which the expected is conveyed to our
imagination. For seven lines, the pleasantness of the castle is
described in terms chosen to give a harmonious impression.
Then suddenly on the spacious green plain a battle is seen to
be taking place. Yet so closely are the knights related to the
green plain that their battle seems to have its own frame to
make it timeless. They might be toy soldiers set out on a toy
plain. This curious emphasis—not primarily on the action as
it might possibly concern Britomart but simply on the pictorial effect—should lead us to ponder on the peculiarity of the
point of view in the poem.

Throughout the poem, Spenser's habit of dividing up an
action into its phases and describing each as a self-contained
scene creates an effect of stillness. As details are added in the
course of the stanza, they appear to be present simultane-
ously in our minds as they must have been in the poet's. This
is that "sleight of mind" of which Leigh Hunt speaks when he
tells how the poet strikes an image on the mind of the reader
"as a face is struck on a mirror"[20] and of which Coleridge,
praising Milton, writes: "This is creation rather than painting,
or if painting, yet such, and with such co-presence of the
whole picture flashed at once upon the eye, as the sun paints
in a camera obscura."[21] Instead of trying to reproduce objects
by describing them with all "their visible properties," the
poet captures the reader's confidence in the reality of his
image by giving it that self-consistency that all true works of
the imagination possess. It is, after all, the integrity of the

image that matters, so that though the poet seems to pass from one detail to another, in reality the whole image remains intact, a conception in its creator's mind which he by subtle hints communicates to his reader.

This effect is perhaps stronger for the simpler narrative images of the poem than for the more highly patterned set pieces, such as the description of Radigund, but the voice of the narrator helps to persuade the reader that even the most elaborate word-painting is not a mere rhetorical display piece but reflects the actual appearance of someone in the fiction. Emblematic images, such as the portrait of Fidelia, may also take on a life of their own in spite of the fact that they do not play a very active part in the story. Again the poet alludes to an image in his own mind rather than to some manuscript illumination:

> She was araied all in lilly white,
> And in her right hand bore a cup of gold,
> With wine and water fild up to the hight,
> In which a serpent did himselfe enfold,
> That horrour made to all that did behold;
> But she no whitt did chaunge her constant mood:
> And in her other hand she fast did hold
> A booke that was both signd and seald with blood,
> Wherin darke things were writt, hard to be understood.
>
> (1.10.13)

The vitality of the image derives partly from the "lilly white" raiment and the "cup of gold"; partly from the horror of the serpent and the book "signd and seald with blood." These latter features are in direct contrast with the figure of Fidelia with her serenity of countenance. A painter who would try to represent the image would have the difficulty not only of making his colors luminous but also of making the serpent, book, and Fidelia herself as expressive as the poetic description. Its apparent motionlessness, as of a picture, allows the reader to meditate upon it and understand its significance. In overcoming the limitations of his medium to create a picture, the poet has at the same time pointed to what the painter in his turn must try to depict: that is, the inner significance of things by means of bodily forms.

As an artist of the eye, expressed in poetry, Spenser is receptive to the world of visual experience; what impinges on his inner sight becomes important both as picture and as impetus to action. It may be as ordinary as Una's wandering through "deserts wyde" until

> at length she found the troden gras,
> In which the tract of peoples footing was,
> Under the steepe foot of a mountaine hore:
> The same she followes, till at last she has
> A damzell spyde slow footing her before,
> That on her shoulders sad a pot of water bore.
>
> (1.3.10)

Here there is no color, no lighting effects, but after the undifferentiated and uninhabited wilderness, the girl with the pot of water on her shoulders attracts our gaze as she attracts Una's. The break between stanzas marks the pause to dwell upon the image before it becomes part of the action and breaks its form as the girl breaks her pitcher at the sight of Una's lion. On the other hand, the image may be as complex as Acrasia's gown, for which similes are needed to convey the effect because simple noun-adjective combinations will not suffice:

> And was arayd, or rather disarayd,
> All in a vele of silke and silver thin,
> That hid no whit her alablaster skin,
> But rather shewd more white, if more might bee:
> More subtile web Arachne cannot spin,
> Nor the fine nets, which oft we woven see
> Of scorched deaw, do not in th' ayre more lightly flee.
>
> (2.12.77)

The net and web comparisons of course add for the alert
reader a moral caution against the trap Acrasia has set, but
they also confirm the artistic beauty of her raiment. An eye so
inclined as this one to translate all visual experience into
pattern must needs see the world as art, but need not, finally,
accept art as guarantee of probity.

But so many are Spenser's references to artistic illusion
that he must have been fascinated by its ambiguities. To him
the effects of art are magical, yet he is also always thinking of
an art beyond art. Sometimes it is nature which represents
this transcendence of art; for example, in his descriptions of
the Medway, Nature's pavilion and carpet of flowers, or
Britomart's hair. At other times, he seems to want to go beyond nature herself to picture something not made of mortal
materials, such as the cloth of state over Mercilla:

> All over her a cloth of state was spred,
> Not of rich tissew, nor of cloth of gold,
> Nor of ought else that may be richest red,
> But like a cloud, as likest may be told,
> That her brode spreading wings did wyde unfold;
> Whose skirts were bordred with bright sunny beams,
> Glistring like gold, amongst the plights enrold,
> And here and there shooting forth silver streames,
> Mongst which crept litle angels through the glittering
>   gleames.
>
> Seemed those litle angels did uphold
> The cloth of state, and on their purpled wings
> Did beare the pendants, through their nimblesse bold.
>   (5.9.28–29)

This cloth of state is "like a cloud" but is not a cloud, any
more than it is an ordinary piece of cloth. So far does
Spenser's imagination outstrip nature, as well as what he calls
"idle craftsmans skill." His use of analogy here, as so often in
the poem, uses visible things to suggest the invisible, for the

true realm of the poet is what is present only to the mind's eye, like Merlin's pictures in *Orlando Furioso,* which were "painted without a brush."

It is fitting that Alma's parlor, the heart, should have no pictures at all:

That was with royall arras rightly dight,
In which was nothing pourtrahed nor wrought,
Not wrought nor pourtrahed, but easie to be thought.

(2.9.33)

In this, the seat of feeling, there is a form of understanding without images. The very blankness of the red tapestry is more striking than the images which adorn the first two rooms of Alma's tower, those of Phantastes and Reason: the first, consisting of fantastic images, such as centaurs and fiends; the second, of pictures of professional men and symbols of the arts and sciences. But in Alma's parlor, where so emphatically "nothing [is] pourtrahed nor wrought / Not wrought nor pourtrahed," Spenser once again seems to be using the *paragone* to suggest that there are limits to what the painter or sculptor can depict.

The greater imaginative freedom of the poet is demonstrated everywhere in the poem but nowhere more beautifully than in the vision of the Graces dancing. For a painter to represent "an hundred naked maidens lilly white, / All raunged in a ring, and dauncing in delight" would seem all but impossible, and as if to prove the point, Spenser has them vanish. But the vision, while it lasts, perplexes Calidore, as all illusions do:

[he] wist not what to weene;
Whether it were the traine of Beauties Queene,
Or nymphes, or faeries, or enchaunted show,
With which his eyes mote have deluded beene.

(6.10.17)

Earlier, we have seen similar uncertainty expressed over illusionistic effects in both art and nature, including the ivory waves of the gate to the Bower of Bliss and the real waves of the River Thames. This uncertainty, which Calidore is unable to tolerate, is simply reason's response to the fluidity of the imaginative experience.

It may be that Spenser was so fascinated by illusion because it seems to represent the loosening of rigid categories, such as those which separate the visible from the invisible, or painting from poetry. Aware as always of the inadequacy of both paint and language, he does not attempt to define everything: Mercilla's magical cloth of state or Sir Calidore's vision are what they are, hinting at a divine blessing but not elucidating it in too definite a fashion. Nevertheless, Spenser believes in providing a framework for these visions, for by delimiting his field in the form of schematic structure, he can give some kind of order to what would otherwise be too chaotic for beauty.

Having affirmed the value of Calidore's vision and therefore of the poetic illusion, Spenser now reminds us of its fragility. As Guyon's angel "vanisht quite away," so the Graces "vanisht all away." Like the spider's web, the poetic illusion may be torn asunder "with least wynd." We are made to understand that there are always two parties to an illusion: the artist and his audience. The storyteller can only do so much to make us see his pictures, and the rest is up to us; we can cause the images to vanish just as readily as Calidore put the Graces to flight. But the true miracle of the poem, which is also the miracle of the dancing Graces, is that Spenser was able to find the right words to speak to his readers' pictorial imaginations, not in order to make photocopies in our minds, but to arouse by sympathy an illusion of seeing, which yet is dependent upon the poet's words for its renewal.

NOTES

1. Hoskins, *Directions for Speech and Style,* p. 42.
2. Philostratus, *Life of Apollonius,* 2:79.
3. Ibid., 1:175.
4. Ibid., 1:179.
5. *The Works of Lucian of Samosata,* trans. H. W. Fowler and F. G. Fowler (Oxford, 1905), 3:23.
6. Mazzoni, "On the Defense of the Comedy," selections in Gilbert, *Literary Criticism,* p. 363.
7. Junius, *Painting of the Ancients,* I.4.6.
8. Ibid. Cf. Albert B. Lord, *The Singer of Tales* (Cambridge, Mass., 1960): "The living eye of the singer's imagination moves in the theme of dressing a hero or in that of caparisoning a horse in the natural order of the action being described" (p. 92). Lord frequently comments on the skill "in fashioning descriptions" which is vital to oral epic.
9. See, for example, such articles as: Rosemond Tuve, "Spenser and Some Pictorial Conventions," *SP,* 37 (1940), 149–76; rpt. in *Essays by Rosemond Tuve,* ed. Thomas P. Roche (Princeton, 1970); F. Hard, "Spenser's Clothes of 'Arras and of Tours,'" *SP,* 27 (1930), 162–85; H. W. Hintz, "The Elizabethan Entertainment and *The Faerie Queene,*" *PQ,* 14 (1935), 83–90.
10. Arnold Williams discusses this style in his book *Flower on a Lowly Stalk: The Sixth Book of The Faerie Queene* (East Lansing, Mich., 1967), p. 89. See also P. M. Kean, *Chaucer and the Making of English Poetry* (London, 1972), 1:12, and Tuve, *Allegorical Imagery,* p. 377.
11. On Spenser's "perspective," see my commentary on Jonathan Kamholtz's article "Spenser and Perspective" (*JAAC,* 39 [1980], 59–66) in *JAAC,* 40 (1981), 82–84.
12. See Joseph B. Dallett, "Ideas of Sight in *The Faerie Queene,*" *ELH,* 27 (1960), 87–121.
13. Rosemund Tuve refers to Spenser's debt to medieval romance in the creation of such figures as Disdain. See her "Spenser and Some Pictorial Conventions."

14. Paul Alpers makes the point that the hallmark of Spenserian narration is "confidence in locutions which are at the same time understood to be provisional" ("Narration in *The Faerie Queene*," *ELH,* 44 [1977], 27). This phenomenon is put into a historical perspective by John Webster in "Oral Form and Written Craft in Spenser's *Faerie Queene*," *SEL,* 16 (1976), 75–93. He notes that "oral poetry is a rhetorical art in which there is more than normal emphasis on the moment of speech" (p. 84). I find myself in substantial agreement with Webster. On the relation between allegory and oral poetry, see Michael Murrin, *The Veil of Allegory* (Chicago, 1969), pp. 68–70.

15. Aristotle, *Rhetoric,* trans. Lane Cooper, 1356.3, p. 9.

16. See Wayne Booth, *The Rhetoric of Fiction* (Chicago, 1961), on "the guiding presence of the author."

17. Demetrius, *On Style,* p. 451.

18. Longinus, *On the Sublime,* trans. W. Rhys Roberts, XV.2, p. 85.

19. See, for example, Alberti, *On Painting.*

20. Leigh Hunt, *Imagination and Fancy,* 3d. ed. (London, 1846), p. 103.

21. Coleridge, *Biographia Literaria* (New York, 1906), p. 230.

"Eternall Peace"

More than once in the proems to the books of *The Faerie Queene,* Spenser uses a foot metaphor. Referring, for example, to his poem, he speaks of those who can and cannot find their way, "In these strange waies, where never foote did use, / Ne none can find, but who was taught them by the Muse" (6.Proem.2). The mystery of fairyland accurately reflects the mystery of allegory, and so fond is Spenser of dwelling upon this idea that he has his hero Sir Calidore wandering in the same "strange waies":

> "now I begin
> To tread an endlesse trace, withouten guyde,
> Or good direction how to enter in,
> Or how to issue forth in waies untryde,
> In perils strange, in labours long and wide."
> (6.1.6)

But this is the hero in his struggle; the poet, more confidently, can pick up the scent and mock those who cannot "without an hound fine footing trace" (2.Proem.4). We marvel at Spenser's sureness in the ways of the imagination, but then he has asked the Muses, "Guyde ye my footing"

(6.Proem.2). The paradox of his passivity and his schematic patterning of his work is akin to that of the believer who is also a sceptic. He does not trust wholly to the imagination but provides it with forms or structures into which it may flow, for the sake of his art.

Can art be such a powerful impulse with him as I have suggested? In the last chapter, the narrator was viewed as one with a gifted eye, for whom illusion is the narrative goal but ornament the artistic goal. He seems to be a passive receptor but is, in fact, a shaper of visual materials for pictorial effects, and his close look will always reveal decorative detail, for that is what this particular eye loves to dwell upon.

It is a slightly naive eye, which is amazed and full of admiration for workmanship and rich materials. It cannot but love opulence; yet to its wonderment, it finds that all is not well sometimes with the finest of appearances. It appears detached because it is innocent but it is fully responsive to all visual experiences in their affectingness.

But the aesthetic sensibility preoccupied Spenser much earlier, in his poem *Muiopotmos*.[1] A very intuitive poem, it probably was not based on a very clear philosophical conception. Nevertheless, philosophically it may be seen to illustrate the doctrine of the conjunction of opposites. The reason the butterfly Clarion falls is that he is too much the creature of Venus, even to his seeking of her garden. It is not that he is actually faced with a choice between reason and sensuality but that, like all tragic heroes, he is not the creature of perfect balance. He is not yet a transcendent butterfly who would combine pleasure with virtue, vulnerability with strength. But the direction of the poem is not to the rejection of pleasure but to the reconciliation of Venus and Minerva (the art that delights and the art that teaches), both of whom have a part in the creation of a butterfly, the one as an act of revenge, the other as an act of triumph. In making a woven butterfly the highest point of her art, Minerva is paying her tribute to the values of Venus, at least when they are transmuted by art. Spenser's is an enlightened epicureanism. Beauty and pleasure are celebrated in the poem, yet the universe requires an armor that is more than decoration: the armor of God.

It is interesting to note how this poem shows art reflecting about itself, turning back on itself, and delighting in itself. Consider the mirroring of flower petals and wings, real butterfly and embroidered. Like Marvell's bird, the butterfly is waving its wings in the various colored light, which is catching all the reflections. Spenser seems to enjoy the paralleling: art as nature and nature as art, that each may serve as a metaphor for the other. But between the real and the tapestried lies a small but incalculable gulf. The spider's web is not so harmless as the lady's woven work, nor the butterfly so frivolous as a lady's fan. The reality is always a moral situation: the living butterfly becomes emblematic of the human soul as the embroidered one, having no freedom of choice, could not be. What to do with this freedom is the essence of the moral problem. If the correspondence between art and nature means that beauty is the ever-present standard by which to judge all things, yet the question of whether beauty is goodness remains as a particular issue which obsesses Renaissance moralists. Their aesthetic must find a divine sanction.

The problem finds some kind of resolution in *The Faerie Queene* through exploring it with human beings, not insects, and through viewing all things with the eyes of a narrator who is a partisan as well as an artist of the eye. He bows before the mystery of things and can become simple in "contemplation of divinitee." This, we feel, is Spenser himself speaking, expressing his deepest longings and convictions about the ultimate source of beauty.

Art, then, in *The Faerie Queene* is finally concerned not merely with craftsmanship, even the craftsmanship which defines the image. Overtly, it is true, Spenser cannot make any other comment on art than on the skill of the artist: "the sweet wit" of the tapestry designer, or the Bower where "the art which all that wrought appeared in no place." It is only when we are led to see the true significance of ornament that we have in fact a glimpse of the wider context in which art must be judged. Then we can see that, for Spenser, the decorum of art reaches beyond the requirements of either verisimilitude or decorative appropriateness into life. Like Cicero and Tasso, he holds that just as physical beauty is based on health, so decorum with its connotations of artistic beauty must be based on virtue.[2]

On the surface, the "greedie eye" metaphors of *The Faerie Queene* refer only to the intense pleasures of visual experience, but the longing for beauty expressed in these metaphors goes beyond anything that the visible world has to offer. Least of all can the visible world provide anything of enduring beauty: Red Cross, the palmer, Arthur, Calidore, all lose sight of their heavenly visions. The impermanence of the visible, including all the moments of aesthetic enjoyment, is constantly before us, written into the very premises of the poem, so that in the end we are not allowed to cling to images, however finely fashioned, as we may in the more purely elegant world of *Muiopotmos*. In the pagan setting of that poem, there could be no conflict between religion and art because the gods were themselves works of art as well as skilled craftsmen. But in *The Faerie Queene,* divinity is well beyond the limits of art and the representative power of images.

And so we return to the forest of fantasy and submit ourselves once more to the web of illusion, the wholeness to which the rhetorical forms and allegorical design only contribute. There we find that words lose their separateness and that we see what they describe. But, amid the dissolvings and reformings of the illusionistic experience, the honeycomb of structure remains to impart a sense of a pattern of significance beyond the visible. As in Elizabeth Boyle's tapestry, peace rules "Between the spyder and the gentle bee."

NOTES

1. My view of this poem is more fully expressed in my article "*Muiopotmos:* A World of Art." See also pp. 51–52 and 96–97.

2. See ch. 5, n. 33.

Spenser and the Muses

As I hinted at the end of my preface, the Muses have a role to play in *The Faerie Queene* which is beyond the purview of rhetoric. At the same time, they take their place rhetorically within the poem through conventional invocations and through their relationship to the fictitious historical sources upon which Spenser is drawing. As daughters of Memory, they link the poet to the past and to his poetic forebears, like the magnet which, in Plato's metaphor, holds a series of iron rings one to another.[1]

The association of poetry with the Muses at once sets it apart from painting and relates it to a divinity of a particular sort. Although Spenser prepares the ground for Milton by the sacredness he attributes to poetry, his very choice of pagan Muses over a biblical source of interpretation supports his view that the way of poetry is one primarily of delight and beauty, rather than of prophetic exhortation. The ideal courtier recreates his mind in company with the "Sweete Ladie Muses, ladies of delight," much as the Graces dance to the music of Colin Clout "in delight." The Muses, in other words, provide the music for the Graces to dance to. When Spenser occasionally chooses to reject the Muses in his poetry, his reasons have to do with his genre or with a pose that he has adopted for the occasion. At such times, his poetry is too base (*Mother Hubberds Tale*), too mournful even for Melpomene (*Daphnaida*), or too loftily religious (*Hymne of Heavenly Love* and *Hymne of Heavenly Beautie*). For the rest, he gladly seeks their aid in his invention, for the Muses provide that direct link to the divine which is denied to painting.

As the daughters of Memory and Jupiter, or Memory and Apollo, the Muses put the poet in relationship not only to the past with its freight of learning but to the creative spark which will generate something new. Through the "learned sisters," the poet is linked to his artistic ancestors, all the way back to Orpheus. Partly at least the origins of every poem were believed to lie in the traditions established by earlier poets, and the very notion of the genres was bound up with the individual Muses, such as the Muse of Comedy, Tragedy, Epic, or Pastoral. The invocation to the Muses thus asks them to aid the poet in striking the right note, in observing those principles of decorum which constitute the essence of true expression.

Spenser's own references to the Muses frequently point to their association with the various genres and with decorum. Even his rejection of them in *Mother Hubberds Tale* assumes that since he has chosen to use a base style for satire he needs no Muse:

> No Muses aide me needes heretoo to call;
> Base is the style, and matter meane withall.
>
> (ll. 43–44)

When, on the other hand, he wishes an ornamented style, he calls on the Muses for aid:

> Ye learned sisters, which have oftentimes
> Beene to me ayding, other to adorne . . .
> Helpe me mine owne loves prayses to resound.
>
> (*Epithalamion*, 1–3)

Similarly, the April eclogue asks that the Muse assist Colin to blaze the glory of the queen. The importance of particular Muses to particular genres seems like an attempt to systematize, but actual differentiation of function was never absolute and often the Muse required is not specified. For example, the overlapping functions of Clio and Calliope as Muses of virtue and "golden trumpet of eternity" presuppose that both history and pseudohistory or myth preserve the memory of great men. *The Faerie Queene* in its feigned historicity naturally comes under the aegis of Clio, but the line in Book VII "Meanwhile O Clio, lend Calliope thy quill" shows him digressing from the main course of his "historicall fiction" to relate a little myth of place.[2] It is evident that he was prepared to make distinctions between these very similar Muses, if only for the sake of an ornamented transition.

In part, Spenser's insistence on the historicity of his tales is simply adherence to the medieval convention enunciated, for example, by Boccaccio, that epic and romance are, or pretend to be, historical.[3] When he asks Clio to "Lay forth out of thine everlasting scryne / The antique rolles, which there lye hidden still, / Of Faerie knights, and fayrest Tanaquill" (1.Proem.2), he is assigning her the same office that she holds in *Teares of the Muses,* where she says: "So I, that doo all noble feates professe / To register. . . ." But a similar claim is made for all the Muses in his dedicatory sonnet to the Earl of Northumberland:

> The sacred Muses have made alwaies clame
>> To be the nourses of nobility,
>> And registres of everlasting fame,
>> To al that armes professe and chevalry.

These registers are the scrolls to which Spenser is referring in *The Faerie Queene;* they are, in fact, a metaphor for memory,

as we can see by the scrolls that furnish the third chamber of
the mind, that of Eumnestes, in the Castle of Alma:

> His chamber all was hangd about with rolls,
> And old records from auncient times derivd,
> Some made in books, some in long parchment scrolls,
> That were all worm-eaten and full of canker holes.
>
> (2.9.57)

Among the books in this library is one called *Briton Moni-
ments,* in which Prince Arthur reads the history of his race;
Sir Guyon meanwhile learns his origins from another book,
called *Antiquitee of Faery Lond.*[4] The parallel between these
two books reiterates Spenser's contention that fairyland is a
mirror realm for England but it also suggests that his emphasis on the historicity of fairyland goes beyond romance or
epic convention to relativize the realms of both England and
fairyland. Neither is more real than the other: fairyland is not
simply a metaphor for England, but England may be a metaphor for fairyland. History itself is mocked by the scrolls of
fairy chronicle; by asserting the existence of fairyland and its
"antique rolls" or "records permanent," Spenser is giving it
equal existence with England. But he can make this claim
only because he recognizes a higher reality than either England or fairyland.

We may contrast Ariosto's very different attitude to belief
as expressed in the exordium of Canto VII in *Orlando Furioso:*

> He who travels far afield beholds things which lie
> beyond the bounds of belief; and when he returns to tell
> of them, he is not believed, but is dismissed as a liar, for
> the ignorant throng will refuse to accept his work, but
> needs must see with their own eyes, touch with their
> own hands. This being so, I realize that my words will
> gain scant credence where they outstrip the experience

of my hearers. Still, whatever degree of reliance is placed on my word, I shall not trouble myself about the ignorant and mindless rabble: I know that you, my sharp, clear-headed listeners, will see the shining truth of my tale. To convince you, and you alone, is all that I wish to strive for, the only reward I seek.[5]

This is superficially like Spenser's proem to Book II, where he defends the existence of fairyland on grounds that new worlds are constantly being discovered and more will be in the future:[6]

> Why then should witlesse man so much misweene,
> That nothing is, but that which he hath seene?

But whereas Spenser is concerned with the problem of belief, Ariosto is not and dismisses it as of no account. But why should Spenser be concerned with this problem, citing both scrolls and the argument of undiscovered worlds? Undoubtedly because he wants belief for the truths he himself believes in.

Besides mysterious scrolls, Spenser acknowledges another, more ultimate source of authority: the Muse. He would in truth have agreed with Sidney that the poet "citeth not authorities of other histories, but even for his entry calleth the sweet Muses to inspire into him a good invention."[7] In presenting himself as the instrument of a knowledge older and vaster than he is, Spenser invokes the Muse of epic first; then the erotic-chivalrous group of Cupid, Venus, Mars; and finally the queen herself. Thus mythology and history meet, as fairyland and England meet, and from their encounter the poem is born. But the poet is only the mediator between these two worlds, by the grace of God. He has followed "the antique poets historicall" because they represent "just memory," the authentic voice of the Muse. Yet he feels it nec-

essary to defend his enterprise against those who can only
accept history in its most literal sense:

> Right well I wote, most mighty Soveraine,
> That all this famous antique history
> Of some th'aboundance of an ydle braine
> Will judged be, and painted forgery,
> Rather then matter of just memory.
>
> (2.Proem.1)

More confidently and beautifully Milton's Attendant Spirit in
Comus makes the same plea for the truth of poetry:

> I'll tell ye, 'tis not vain or fabulous,
> (Though so esteem'd by shallow ignorance)
> What the sage Poets taught by the heav'nly Muse,
> Storied of old in high immortal verse
> Of dire Chimeras and enchanted Isles,
> And rifted Rocks whose entrance leads to Hell,
> For such there be, but unbelief is blind.
>
> (ll. 513–19)

Quite likely, Milton has Spenser in mind as one of "the sage
Poets taught by the heav'nly Muse."[8]

To learn from the Muse, the poet "close confers" with her;
that is, he withdraws from the world to become receptive to
sacred influences. And yet the Muse is within the poet, as
well as outside: Spenser, like Dante, has his personal source
of inspiration, as well as the impersonal, eternal Muses.[9] But
whether inside or outside the poet, the Muse demands that
he prove faithful to his chosen genre by "masking," as though
dressed for a theatrical role. In the November eclogue, it is
appropriate for Colin Clout to say that his "mornefull Muse"
does not want to mask in mirth but will wear a garb suited to
the season and his state of mind. The October eclogue, on
the other hand, more squarely dwells upon the issue of which

genre the poet should choose, whether his Muse should display herself in heroic, love, pastoral, or tragic poetry. In put-
ting the Muse "on stately stage," under the influence of wine,
Cuddie would be showing her to the world in the accoutrements befitting her, teaching her to "tread aloft in buskins
fine, / With queint Bellona in her equipage!" This theatrical
metaphor is only the most obvious way of saying that whatever Muse the poet elects to follow, it is his duty to make her
recognizably what she is. He owes it to her to give her the
appropriate style and costume. His own private Muse thus
assumes the role of one of the public Muses, displaying "her
fluttering wing" to best advantage.

The opening lines of *The Faerie Queene,* with their allusion
to a change of attire and of musical instrument, are a reminder that Spenser cannot conceive of expression apart
from genre:

> Lo! I the man whose Muse whylome did maske,
> As time her taught, in lowly shephards weeds,
> Am now enforst, a farre unfitter taske,
> For trumpets sterne to chaunge mine oaten reeds.

Later, in the eleventh canto of Book I, he asks that the Muse
come "gently," rather than with "that furious fitt" appropriate
to great wars, that she "a while lett downe that haughtie
string, / And to my tunes thy second tenor rayse, / That I this
man of God his godly armes may blaze" (1.11.7). This lower
strain is more appropriate to the battle of one man, Red
Cross, than it would be to that of an army.[10] Such appeals
suggest that the gift of expression is worthless unless deco-
rously attuned to the subject. But the learning of the Muses,
derived from their mother Memory, ensures that their aid in
invention will always be in keeping with the principles of
great poetry.

No merely mechanical skill will suffice for the poet, who must be able to present his theme in the most arresting way. His choice of genre, important as it is, is nothing without the power to reinvent it by the very novelty of the use to which it is put. Both *The Shepheardes Calender* and *The Faerie Queene*—to mention only Spenser's major works—demonstrate his capacity to devise a scheme which will give a new purpose to the conventions of pastoral and romance. In the light of his achievements, such commendatory poems as the one prefixed to the *Amoretti* take on real significance:

> Ah! Colin, whether on the lowly plaine,
> Pyping to shepherds thy sweete roundelaies,
> Or whether singing, in some lofty vaine,
> Heroick deeds of past or present daies,
> Or whether in thy lovely mistris praise
> Thou list to exercise thy learned quill,
> Thy Muse hath got such grace, and power to please,
> With rare invention, bewtified by skill,
> As who therein can ever joy their fill?

In these lines G. W. Junior first notes some of the genres Spenser adopted and then praises his "rare invention," or new way of conceiving the subject and adorning it with well-chosen words.

If through the Muses the poet has a direct link to Heaven, it is not so with painter or sculptor. Without noting that there are no Muses for these arts, Spenser asks "how can mortall immortalitie give?" (*Ruines of Time*, l. 413). However fine the pyramids, brazen pillars, and shrines "made of the metall most desired," their pomp cannot last. At moments, he seems to equate the fine arts not only with mortality but with the moral depravity of merely earthly splendor. The *Complaints* are dismissive of "stately galleries / Wrought with faire pil-

lours, and fine imageries," because their glory can only be a
vanity.

Yet sometimes even these monuments "which not in paper
writ, / but in prophyre and marble" require the tribute of
memory and words. In spite of Spenser's jeering at "vain
Antiquitie" in his commendatory sonnet on Scanderbeg, with
his reference to "their statues, their colossoes great, / Their
rich triumphall arcks which they did raise, / Their huge pyramids, which do heaven threat," he shares Du Bellay's conviction that it is his duty to "give a second life to dead decayes."
The past glories of Rome demand the poet's evocation, with
the help of the Muses:

> Or that at least I could with pencill fine
> Fashion the pourtraicts of these palacis,
> By paterne of great Virgils spirit divine!
> I would assay with that which in me is
> > To build, with levell of my loftie style,
> > That which no hands can evermore compyle.
>
> > > *(Ruines of Rome,* xxv)

This much the daughters of Memory owe to mortal works.

But the poet as keeper of memory has more important
tasks. Spenser likes to illustrate the power of the Muses by
alluding to the story of Orpheus and Eurydice in its happier
version, and this in turn becomes a metaphor for rescuing a
person's name from oblivion:

> The sevenfold yron gates of grislie Hell,
> And horrid house of sad Proserpina,
> They able are with power of mightie spell
> To breake, and thence the soules to bring awaie
> Out of dread darknesse to eternall day
> And them immortall make, which els would die
> In foule forgetfulness, and nameles lie.
>
> > *(Ruines of Time,* 372–78)

The Muses are the mythmakers, raising not only Hercules and Bacchus to the skies, but also Charlemagne. Besides preserving men's fame, they record wise words:

> But wise wordes taught in numbers for to runne,
> Recorded by the Muses, live for ay.
>
> *(Ruines of Time,* 402–3)

All the values of a classical humanist culture meet in these beings, who stand for history with its moral significance and for beauty with its sisterhood of nymphs and graces. Painting indeed could only become a liberal art through imitating the poets and thereby finding a contact with the Muses, even if only at second hand.[11]

Yet whatever Spenser's rivalry with the painter—explicit in his references to the *paragone* or implicit in all his imagery—this is nothing more than a recognition of the struggle he himself feels to transcend the limits of his own medium and express an inner truth. The Muses represent figuratively the divine transcendence of the struggle represented on an earthly level by the *paragone.*

At the same time, Spenser recognizes a more ultimate *paragone* between the Muses and all the Siren voices of art which have the power to lead the soul astray. He opposes the Muses to the Sirens, by direct allusion in Book II, during Guyon's voyage to the Bower of Bliss, and by implication throughout *The Faerie Queene.* In the allegorization of classical myth, the Sirens traditionally figured as voluptuous desire and the seductive aspect of beauty; Natalis Comes, however, treats the Muses as "the best remedy against all enticement of sensual pleasure," because only they can meet the Sirens on their own ground of sweet music.[12] In *The Divine Comedy,* too, Dante describes a dream to show how it takes a Beatrice-like figure to strengthen even Virgil against the Siren who appears to both of them. Something above reason must come to the hero's rescue to meet this threat. When Dante begins *The Purgatorio,* he therefore invokes the Muses in opposition to the Sirens: "But here let poetry rise again from the dead, O holy Muses, since I am yours; and here let Calliope rise up for a while and accompany my song with that strain which smote the ears of the wretched pies so that they despaired of pardon!"[13] Spenser also has in mind the symbolism of the Sirens and the Muses as representing two kinds of art:

> They were faire ladies, till they fondly striv'd
> With th' Heliconian maides for maystery;
> Of whom they over-comen, were depriv'd
> Of their proud beautie, and th' one moyity
> Transformed to fish, for their bold surquedry;
> But th' upper halfe their hew retayned still,
> And their sweet skill in wonted melody;
> Which ever after they abusd to ill,
> T' allure weake traveillers, whom gotten they did kill.
>
> (2.12.31)

It is not by chance that the allusion to this contest appears here in the canto where, perhaps more than anywhere else in the poem, an evil art seems almost to triumph. But Spenser has reminded us that ultimately it is the heaven-inspired Muses who will win the contest. Sandys in his commentary on *The Metamorphoses* notes that the daughters of Pierius were transformed in their lower parts because they vilifed the gods, "since Poesy, in regard of her originall, inspired into the mind from above, should chiefly, if not onely, be exercised in celebrating their praises; as here exemplified by the Muses."[14]

Only the Muses can provide that sense of decorum which first invented the genres and which continues to reinvent them in the interests of truth. Like Dante, Spenser sides with the Muses not only because he recognizes his own inadequacy as an artist trying to express the inexpressible, but also because he is on the side of the gods, whose praises they sing:

> But vaine it is to thinke, by paragone
> Of earthly things, to judge of things divine.
> (*Colin Clouts Come Home Againe,* 344–45)

NOTES

1. Plato, *Ion,* 533C, 535E.

2. On the controversy over whether Clio or Calliope is the presiding Muse of *The Faerie Queene,* I find myself in agreement with H. E. Lotspeich, *Classical Mythology in the Poetry of Edmund Spenser* (1932; rpt. New York, 1965), pp. 84–85; and with Patrick O'Dyer Spurgeon, "Spenser's Muses," *Renaissance Papers* (1969), ed. G. W. Williams (Durham, N.C., 1970), pp. 15–23. Clio's name, which comes from the Greek *cleos,* meaning *glory,* is particularly apt for the celebration of Gloriana. The name also appears in Cleopolis (1.10.58–59). For further discussion of the points at issue, see "The Muse of the *Faerie Queene,*" *Spenser Variorum,* 1:506–15. But perhaps the truth of the matter is that in the poem Calliope, the Muse of epic poetry, wears the dress of Clio, the Muse of history.

3. Charles G. Osgood, *Boccaccio on Poetry* (Princeton, 1930), pp. 48–49.

4. On the significance of the chronicles, see Harry Berger, Jr., *The Allegorical Temper* (New Haven, 1957), ch. 4.

5. Ariosto, *Orlando Furioso,* trans. Guido Waldman (Oxford, 1974), 7.1. For a full comparison between the narrators of Ariosto and Spenser, see Robert M. Durling, *The Figure of the Poet in Renaissance Epic* (Cambridge, Mass., 1965).

6. For an interesting treatment of Spenser's fairyland, see Michael Murrin, "The Rhetoric of Fairyland," in *The Rhetoric of Renaissance Poetry,* ed. Thomas O. Sloan and Raymond B. Waddington (Berkeley, 1974), pp. 73–95.

7. Sidney, *Apology for Poetry,* p. 124.

8. Not only did Milton refer to "our sage and serious Poet *Spenser,*" (*Areopagitica,* in *Complete Prose Works of John Milton,* ed. Sirluck, p. 516) but he also seems to be alluding to Spenser in *Il Penseroso* when he refers to great bards who

> In sage and solemn tunes have sung,
> Of Turney's and of Trophies hung;
> Of Forests, and inchantments drear,
> Where more is meant than meets the ear.
>
> (ll. 117–21)

9. "O Muse, o alto ingegno, or m'aiutate; / o mente che scrivesti ciò ch'io vidi" (*Inferno* 2.7–8). On the history of the Muses and the development of the poet's apostrophe to his own soul in late antiquity, see Curtius, *European Literature and the Latin Middle Ages,* pp. 228–46.

10. It is Red Cross's deeds of arms which will be blazed. His individual exploits are contrasted with the wars "Twixt that great Faery Queene and Paynim King, / That with their horror heven and earth did ring"—a theme reiterated in Red Cross's statement that he must leave Una in order to serve the Faerie Queene "in warlike wize, / Gainst that proud Paynim King that works her teene" (1.12.18). Spenser may have intended to conclude his epic with an account of this war.

11. See P. O. Kristeller, "The Modern System of the Arts," in *Renaissance Thought,* II (New York, 1965), pp. 173–74.

12. Natalis Comes, *Mythologiae* (Frankfurt, 1581), VII.xv, p. 777; "vt optimum creditae sint remedium aduersus omnes voluptatum illecebras." On the nonclassical musical contest between the Muses and Sirens and the conflation of the Sirens with the Pierides, see John P. Cutts, "Spenser's Mermaids," *ELN,* 5 (1968), 250–56.

13. Dante, *The Purgatorio,* trans. John D. Sinclair (Oxford, 1948). The original reads:

Ma qui la morta poesi resurga,
o sante Muse, poi che vostro sono;
e qui Calliope alquanto surga,
seguitando il mio canto con quel sono
di cui le Piche misere sentiro
lo colpo tal, che disperar perdono.

(Purg. 1.7–12)

14. Sandys, *Ovid's Metamorphosis* (1632), ed. Karl K. Hulley and Stanley T. Vandersall (Lincoln, Nebr., 1970), p. 263. The older Milton in one of his typical rejections of the Muses identifies them with the Sirens: his great work, he says, is not "to be obtained by the invocation of Dame Memory and her Siren daughters, but by devout prayer to that eternall Spirit who can enrich with all utterance and knowledge" ("Reason of Church-Government," in *Complete Prose Works of John Milton,* I, ed. Don M. Wolfe [New Haven, 1953], pp. 820–21). But for Sidney, as for Spenser, the Muses remain the supreme metaphor for poetic inspiration, and it is only the enemies of poetry, according to Sidney, who would identify it with "a siren's sweetness drawing the mind to the serpents tale of sinful fancy" (*Apology for Poetry,* p. 123).

Illustrations

Figure 1. Jacob Cats, *Silenus or Proteus* (Amsterdam, 1619), in *Emblemata* (Amsterdam, 1620), Plate XXVI, p. 53.

The motto and poems have been omitted because they do not have a bearing on my argument. Cats may well have borrowed this plate showing a well-ordered Renaissance garden from some other source and adapted it to his own purpose. Certainly, the same plate, reversed, appears in an edition of his collected works (Amsterdam, 1658) with a new motto and new poems.

Minus Cats's various mottoes and poems, the plate serves to illustrate the passages from Seneca and Lyly cited on pp. 2–4. It might equally illustrate Castiglione's recommendation that the courtier be like the bee in imitating the best models available to him: "And even as in green meadows the bee flits about among the grasses robbing the flowers, so our Courtier must steal his grace from those who seem to him to have it, taking from each the part that seems most worthy of praise" (*The Book of the Courtier*, p. 126). Poet and courtier alike perfect their art by following the example of the bee.

Figure 2. Jacob Bruck, *Emblemata Moralia & Bellica.* The French edition published in Strasbourg in 1616 contains the following development of the motto *Usu Diverso:*

> La mouche porte miel, L'araigne filandriere
> Succent diversement une fleur printaniere
> L'une y prend son poison, l'autre son miel succrin
> Ou le bien ou le mal espere la personne
> Selon que son esprit à l'un des deux l'addonne
> Mesme chose peut bien avoir plus d'une fin.

The plate shows two pairs of lovers, one behaving immodestly beneath the spider and its web, surrounded by what appears to be an ivy trail. The other couple walks by the row of beehives, to which the man points, as though to instruct his friend on the virtuous life, while overhead the bees are shown flying back and forth between the rose bush and the hives. In Geoffrey Whitney's similar emblem, the spider and the bee represent the opposite effects of the Scriptures on good and evil readers. See *A Choice of Emblemes* (1586), p. 51. The metaphor was of equal use to stand for two ways of reading Ovid's *Metamorphoses.* Arthur Golding in his preface to his translation (1567) notes:

> Then take theis woorkes as fragrant flowers most full of
> pleasant juice,
> The which the Bee conveying home may put to wholesome
> use:
> And which the spyder sucking on to poyson may convert,
> Through venym spred in all her limbes and native in her hart.
>
> (ll. 163–66)

The spider and the bee thus represent moral differences. From the same flower, the spider takes poison, while the bee takes honey, each according to his spirit or inclination. As in all emblems, there is the possibility of multiple meanings or applications. Even the opposition of these two insects, treated didactically in Bruck, Golding, and Whitney, can turn into a metaphor for the reconciliation and union of lovers, as in Spenser's sonnet 71. See p. 7.

Usu diverso diversa insecta probantur:
Colligit hac virus, colligit illa favum.
Ut cuiq; est animus, quoq; sic operatur; et una
Usus diversos Res habet, atq; capit.

21.

Figure 3. Hendrick Goltzius, *Touch* (circa 1578).

In the engraving reproduced here, Goltzius is possibly making use of a Cleopatra figure as a historicizing allegory. The woman is being bitten on one hand by a snake, while with the other hand she confronts a drenching rain. The snake and the rain represent effects of touch; the other attributes are a turtle and a spider web, both traditional emblems of sensitivity to touch. Below is an inscription, the first line of which refers to illicit love, as though to confirm the allusion to Cleopatra: "Take care not to be moved by the illicit sense of Venus, / And let the lawful couch be your remedy."

Curiously, the pose of Goltzius's *Touch* bears some resemblance to that of Lucretia in Marcantonio Raimondi's famous engraving after Raphael. The virtuous Lucretia is of course the exact opposite of Cleopatra, but the fact that they both committed suicide might have suggested the parallel to Goltzius. At any rate, in his latest drawing of Touch, now in the Pierpont Morgan Library, he showed Lucretia stabbing herself, surrounded by the same attributes of turtle and spider web. He thus moves from the pangs of illicit love to the sufferings of a virtuous love that has been violated.

The use of the turtle as an attribute of touch may be compared with Shakespeare's use of the snail image in *Love's Labors Lost* (IV.iii.334–35) and in *Venus and Adonis* (ll. 1033–34). As for the spider web, its fragility was a common theme of poets. Spenser (p. 7) and Sidney (p. 13 n. 7) allude to it in this way. Sir John Davies even makes the spider and its web the central image of his poem on "Feeling" in his *Nosce Teipsum* (1599, ll. 1057–64):

> Lastly, the feeling power, which is Life's root,
> Through every living part itself doth shed,
> By sinews which extend from head to foot
> And like a net all o'er the body spread.
>
> Much like a subtle spider which doth sit
> In middle of her web, which spreadeth wide,
> If aught do touch the utmost thread of it,
> She feels it instantly on every side.

Tactus

Illicito Cypriæ sensu moueare, caueto,
Legitim usq; tibi sit medicina thorus.

Figure 4. Veronese, *Industry* (detail), Sala del Collegio, Palazzo Ducale, Venice (1576–78).

The allegorical figure holding up a spider's web is one of a series of personifications painted by Veronese for the ceiling of the Sala del Collegio in the Doges' Palace. The others include representations of Recompense, Purity, Mildness, Fidelity, Moderation, Vigilance, and Public Felicity—a collection of civic and religious virtues. The one shown here is both the most beautiful and the most enigmatic. The woman gazes up at the spider in his work of ceaseless and fine industry; the web he has been weaving is attached to a stick she holds in one hand, while with the other hand she holds the web at arm's length up to the sky. (The web suggests a link to Minerva, who, as goddess of "spinning, weaving, and curious working of cloth," was patroness of industry. See Fig. 5 and note.) At her feet is a basket with woven fabrics and a pair of scissors. Weaving has here been turned into a symbol of all the technical skills of the Venetian Republic. The uppermost basket is itself woven, like an echo of the spider's web.

Spenser too is impressed by woven baskets. In his *Prothalamion,* the nymphs each carry "a little wicker basket, / Made of fine twigs entrayld curiously" (ll. 24–25). More important, in his *Muiopotmos,* he explicitly compares the woven work of damsels with the spider's web. See the passage quoted on p. 6.

Opposite Veronese's figure of Industry is Purity, with her attribute, the ermine, illustrating the import of the inscription *Numquam Derelicta,* that religion is never to be forgotten in the pursuit of earthly goals. Quite naturally, Purity is more withdrawn into herself than Industry is. The two figures are also contrasted in the direction of their gaze: while Purity looks down, Industry looks up, so that there is, for each figure, a balancing of the claims of this world and the next. The simplicity and humility of innocence, represented by the ermine, is contrasted too with the intricacy of the spider's web. No longer a mere schematic web, as in the emblem books, it realizes the beauty described by Philostratus in his account of a painted spider web (*Imagines,* II.28). Indeed, so splendid is Veronese's web that the usual relationship between allegorical figure and attribute is reversed, and the allegorical figure now plays a supporting role.

Figure 5. Richard Haydocke, title page for his translation of Giovanni Paolo Lomazzo, *A Tracte containing the Artes of curious Paintinge Caruinge & Buildinge* (Oxford, 1598).

When Haydocke made his translation of the first five books of Lomazzo's *Trattato dell'Arte de la pittura* (2d ed., 1585), he published it with a frontispiece of his own design. He included a self-portrait, as well as the portrait of Lomazzo from the title page of the first book of the *Trattato*. But the rest consists of mythological allusions to the "Artes of Curious Painting Caruing Building." Sculpture, represented by Prometheus, and architecture, represented by Dedalus, together with the abuse of these arts, are shown in the lower part of the page. In the upper part is painting, divided into two aspects, with Juno on the right, representing color and light with her peacock and eye-topped scepter, and Minerva, representing *disegno,* on the left. Here, too, Haydocke is at pains to indicate the misuse of art, and for this purpose the story of Minerva's triumph over Arachne is appropriate. Minerva, wearing armor, holds a cloak in her left hand, with a border of olive, her tree, representing her victory over Arachne. On the side toward which she looks there is also a large spider web in the corner, to stand for the *disegno* of which she is the patroness. On the left, she holds a lance, and on this side, from which she turns away, is a smaller, less elegant web, with two spiders hanging from it by a thread. A dragon below is apparently leaping up at the lower spider. The two spiders joined by a thread may illustrate the words of Minerva to Arachne, as reported by Ovid: "Live, wicked girl; live on, but hang forever, / And, just to keep you thoughtful for the future, / This punishment shall be enforced for always / On all your generations" (VI.136–38) (trans. Rolfe Humphries). As for the presence of the dragon, it may allude to the serpent which as an attribute of Athene was placed next to her huge statue on the Acropolis. Finally, in folklore, there was a traditional enmity between spider and serpent—and the dragon is simply a winged serpent. (See p. 5.) The angry dragon of Haydocke's title page probably suggests the watchful wisdom which fends off wicked opponents, including the envious. Minerva is thus defended on this side, not only by her lance but by her

dragon. Nevertheless, the fact that there is a web on her undefended side strongly suggests that it is an attribute for her own surpassing skill in needlework and design.

Undoubtedly, there is an ambiguity in the attitudes expressed toward the spider in Renaissance writings, summed up by Thomas Moffett in his *Theater of Insects,* translated and included in Edward Topsell's *The History of Four-Footed Beasts and Serpents* (1658). He expresses an admiration for the spider for its courage in "descending down perpendicularly to the Serpents head" to attack it, and notes that both its amazing courage and its fine workmanship, which he calls better than any tapestry, point to "the finger of God working in his poor and weak Creatures" (pp. 783, 785). But just as Moffett gives the credit to God alone, so Haydocke's message is that the power of the artist comes from above and should be used under God. He includes an inscription from Ecclesiastes under his title: "In the handes of the skilfull shall the worke be approved." By this he means not only approval by the best human judges but by the gods.

Figure 6. Hendrick Goltzius, *The Judgment of Midas* (1590).

The following engraving is a *copia* on the scene described by Ovid in *Metamorphoses,* XI. 156 ff. On the right, Midas already wears the ass's ears which were the penalty of his wrong judgment in preferring the music of Pan to the music of Apollo. The other judge of this musical contest was Tmolus, the mountain god, shown here wearing an oak wreath. Apollo is in the center, surrounded by Minerva and the nine Muses, complete with their attributes. Ovid does not include Minerva and the Muses in this story, but the similar story of the contest between Apollo and Marsyas frequently included Minerva (because it was she who invented and subsequently discarded the flute, which was the instrument of Marsyas); and where Minerva is, the Muses cannot be far behind. (See, for example, *The Myths of Hyginus,* CLXV, on Marsyas.) They participate in the judgment on all who are foolish enough to prefer "illiterate rusticity" to "the divine endowments of art and nature" (Sandys, *Ovid's Metamorphoses,* p. 524). See the Excursus above on the roles of the Muses. Minerva as goddess of the arts is mentioned on pp. 11 and 51–52. See also the notes to Figs. 4 and 5.

The inscription beneath the picture reads as follows:

"The Arcadian Half-goat strives, with Tmolus as judge, to match his marshy reeds against the lyre of the Thymbraean god [= Apollo]. The Satyrs stand around, swift runners with their cloven hooves, and watch with amazement the strivings of their own Pan. The child of Leto [= Apollo] stands with shining locks, equipped with his ivory quill: close by are those sacred powers, the Muses. The mad Lydian awards the palm to the Goat-footed One: Tmolus gives it to you, Phoebus, for you keep watchful care over Pindus and Haemus. Stupid things please fools: they reject the choice, and leaving his last the cobbler does poorly to criticize Apelles. He whose heart hides a dull mind thunders loudly: it is because of your ignorance that you, Bavius, make such noise, and you, stupid little Maevius. True art is modest and quiet, leaving braying clarions to wafflers with their swelling verbiage."

General Index

Adjectives, 75, 104, 132–33, 169
Adjuncts, 73, 125–26, 152. *See also* Circumstances
Alberti, Leon Battista, 26, 41, 101, 112, 188n19
Allegory, 9, 11–12, 15–17, 25, 86–88, 92n23, 94–95, 101, 117, 188n14, 189
Alpers, Paul, 90n7, 188n14
Alpers, Svetlana L., 64n17
Apelles, 42, 61–62
Ariosto, Lodovico, 8, 21, 91n19, 115, 179, 185, 197–98
Aristotle, 41, 127, 154n16, 174

Bacon, Francis, 128
Baldovinetti, Alessio, 102, 119n17
Baxandall, Michael, 32n10, 121n30
Bembo, Pietro, 65n19

Bender, John, 90n9
Berger, Harry, Jr., 205n4
Boccaccio, Giovanni, 120n24, 196
Booth, Wayne, 188n16
Bowra, C. M., 153n23
Boyle, Elizabeth, 9, 13n6, 193
Browne, Sir Thomas, 155n40
Buoni, Thomas, 98–99, 100
Burke, Edmund, 72

Cain, Thomas H., 120n19, 155n28
Castiglione, Baldassare, 45, 119n13
Castiglione, Sabbia di, 42
Cervantes, Miguel de, 35
Chastel, André, 26, 119n11
Chaucer, Geoffrey, 28, 173, 176–79
Cicero, 43, 61, 192
Cinthio, Giraldi, 72, 89n1
Circumstances, 76, 82, 91n19, 130, 152. *See also* Adjuncts

Clements, R. J., 13n*3*
Cohen, Gillian, 90n*9*, 154n*18*
Coignet, Matthieu, 41
Coleridge, Samuel Taylor, 89,
    181
Colonna, Francesco, 111
Comes, Natalis, 203
Cooper, Lane, 120n*20*
Craig, Martha, 154n*25*
Curtius, Ernst Robert, 67n*35*,
    92n*26*, 156n*40*, 206n*9*

Dante, 17, 36, 130, 173,
    203–4
Decorum, 24, 104, 114,
    126–27, 133, 139, 142,
    147–48, 151, 155n*32*, 165,
    192, 195, 204
Demetrius, 120n*25*, 142, 175
Descriptive schemes:
    cronographia, 83, 135–39;
    icon, 84; *pragmatographia*,
    80–83; *prosopographia*,
    75–78; *prosopopoeia*, 84–85;
    topographia, 78–79;
    topothesia, 80. See also Epic
    simile
Dolce, Lodovico, 42, 107, 115,
    128
Donne, John, 54
Doran, Madeleine, 118n*2*
Dürer, Albrecht, 42
Du Bellay, Joachim, 58, 202
Durling, Robert A., 205n*5*

Efficacy, 71, 124, 129. See also
    Enargeia
E. K., 17, 67n*32*, 110–11, 117
Ekphrasis, 42–44, 54, 64n*17*,
    69–70, 78, 88

Emblem, 29–30, 45, 114–15,
    126, 150, 168, 179, 182
Enargeia, 72, 130–31. See also
    Efficacy
Encomium, 120n*19*, 149. See
    also Descriptive schemes,
    prosopographia
Epic, 17–18, 24, 103, 147–48,
    165, 196
Epic simile, 85–86, 135
Equicola, Mario, 102
Erasmus, Desiderius, 104,
    130
Evans, Joan, 13n*6*
Expressiveness, 123, 134–35,
    141, 144–45, 150, 152,
    153n*8*, 155n*39*, 182, 200.
    See also Decorum

Fantasy, 11, 17, 19–20, 28,
    30, 37, 158–59, 161, 185.
    See also Imagination
Faral, Edmond, 73, 139
Ficino, Marsilio, 14n*9*, 26,
    65n*23*, 100, 106
Formulas, 23, 74, 129, 132,
    139–40, 174, 176–77, 181.
    See also Stylization
Fracastoro, Girolamo, 100, 104
Fraunce, Abraham, 97–98,
    125–26
Freeman, Rosemary, 122n*42*
Frye, Northrop, 153n*3*

Genre, 17, 23–24, 96, 114,
    165, 194–95, 199–202, 204
Ghiberti, Lorenzo, 42
Gombrich, E. H., xii–xiii,
    66n*30*, 106, 122n*42*,
    154n*15*, 155n*39*

Gracián, Balthasar, 143
G. W. Junior, 201

Hamilton, A. C., x–xi,
66n25
Harington, Sir John, 45,
127–28
Harvey, Gabriel, 31
Hardison, O. B., Jr., 120n19
Hathaway, Baxter, 13n7
Herbert, George, 146
Hermogenes, 70
Hieatt, A. Kent, 67nn33,
34
Homer, 4, 43, 172
Horace, 153n13
Hoskins, John, 108
Hughes, John, 20
Hunt, Leigh, 181

Illusion, 4, 8–9, 35, 42, 45,
47, 55–56, 66–67n31, 73,
92–94, 157, 184–86, 193
Imagination, 73, 125, 130–31,
158, 161, 163, 185, 190. *See
also* Fantasy
Imitation: of nature, 51–55,
160; of other writers, 3–4,
55
Invention, 12, 16, 25, 102,
195, 198, 200–201
Inexpressibility, 60–63, 69

Jack, A. A., 86
James, Henry, 70
Jonson, Ben, 38
Junius, Franciscus, 10, 161

Kamholtz, Jonathan, 187n11
Kristeller, P. O., 206n11

Langer, Suzanne, 92n25
Laurentius, Andreas, 125
Lechner, Joan Marie, 31n5
Lee, Rensselaer W., 63–64n4
Leonardo da Vinci, 38, 40–41,
131–32
Lessing, G. E., 115, 122n44,
155n38
Lewis, C. S., 32n11, 33n18,
154n23
Lomazzo, Giovanni Paolo, 132
Longinus, 136, 175
Lord, Albert B., 187n8
Lotspeich, H. E., 205n2
Lucian, 160
Lyly, John, 2, 13n6, 65n20

MacCaffrey, Isabel, 66–67n31
Malatesta, Gioseppe, 109
Marvell, Andrew, 191
Mazzeo, J. A., 65n23
Mazzoni, Jacopo, 160–61
Memory, 124–25, 194–96,
198, 202, 207n14
Metaphor, 50, 63, 75,
112–13, 165–66, 173, 197,
207n14
Michelangelo, 28
Milton, John, 107, 115,
122n43, 181, 199, 206n8,
207n14
Minturno, Antonio Sebastiano,
22
Mirror, 11, 34–38, 46
Murrin, Michael, 188n14,
205n6

Narrator, 9–10, 129, 164–75,
182
Nashe, Thomas, 95

Ong, Walter J., 120n26
Ornament: embroidery and
  tapestry, 4–8, 13n6, 51–53,
  66n28, 96, 102, 195; gold
  and jewels, 47–48, 103,
  105–7, 112, 120n20, 172;
  nature, 44–45, 57–58,
  97–99, 105, 109–11, 141;
  order, 3, 24, 26, 95, 100,
  116, 143; significance of, 93,
  100–101, 120n25, 143, 192;
  variety, 58, 107–12, 117,
  179. *See also* Stylization
Ovid, 52–53, 66n28, 161

Panofsky, Erwin, ix–x, 67n36
Paragone, 38, 46, 49, 59, 61,
  63, 65n19, 161, 185, 203
Patterson, Annabel, 155n32
Peacham, Henry (1546–1634),
  71, 75–85 *passim,* 106, 124,
  133
Peacham, Henry
  (1576–1643?), 103–4
Periphrasis, 83, 136, 138
Plato, 35, 55, 63, 194
Philostratus, 43, 78, 158
Pliny the Elder, 12n1
Plutarch, 14n11
Pope-Hennessey, John,
  119n17
Puttenham, George, 17, 37,
  42–43, 70, 102, 106,
  123–24, 148

Quintilian, 43, 101, 112,
  129–30

Raleigh, Sir Walter, 62
Raphael, 62, 65n19

Rhetorica ad Herennium,
  120n20, 124–25
Richardson, George, 153
Rix, H. D., 91n18
Romance, 8, 9, 17–18, 20–25,
  30, 146–47, 169, 174–75,
  196

Sandys, George, 204
Seneca, 2
Shakespeare, William, 35, 39,
  40, 44, 53, 69, 121n38, 135
Shearman, John, 65n20
Sherry, Richard, 78
Sidney, Sir Philip, 13n7, 16, 39,
  41, 66n24, 67n36, 68–69,
  87–88, 93, 99, 110, 112,
  124, 148, 158, 165, 207n14
Spenser, Edmund: *Amoretti,* 7,
  61, 108; *Colin Clouts Come
  Home Againe,* 175, 205;
  Dedicatory Sonnets, 4, 62,
  196; *Epithalamion,* 195;
  Hymne in Honour of Beautie,
  48, 61, 67n31, 94; *Hymne of
  Heavenly Beautie, xi,* 35, 62,
  63, 106; *Letter to Raleigh,*
  15–16, 68, 93; *Mother
  Hubberds Tale,* 84, 195;
  Muiopotmos, 5–6, 51–52,
  66n24, 95–96, 117–18,
  190–92; *Ruines of Rome,*
  202; *Ruines of Time,* 4,
  201–3 *passim; Shepheardes
  Calender,* 2, 37, 71, 110,
  175, 196, 199–200; *Teares
  of the Muses,* 4, 5, 196;
  Virgils Gnat, 5; *Visions of the
  Worlds Vanitie,* 5. *See also*
  Index to *The Faerie Queene*

Spurgeon, Patrick O'Dyer,
205n2
Stanza, 30, 74, 95, 116, 178
Stewart, Dugald, 89
Structure, 2–3, 9, 11, 16, 20,
26–28, 30–31, 88–89,
100–101, 107, 118n2,
118–19n5, 123, 152, 190,
193
Stylization, 23–24, 31,
114–15, 150–52, 157, 177.
See also Formulas
Suger, Abbot, 105–6, 107

Tasso, Torquato, 26, 37, 49,
80, 127–28, 142, 148, 192
Titian, 53, 83
Tuve, Rosemond, xiii, 25,
31n4, 102, 108–9, 155n32,
187n13

Ut pictura poesis, 38, 40–41,
63, 68, 71

Vasari, Giorgio, 43, 45
Vida, Marco Girolamo, 5
Virgil, 5
Vituperatio, 149–51

Webster, John, 188n14
Wittig, Susan, 91n15
Williams, Arnold, 187n10
Williams, Kathleen, 32n17
Wilson, Thomas, 128
Wind, Edgar, 65n23,
121n35

Yates, Frances, 153n5

Zeuxis, 61

Index to *The Faerie Queene*

BOOK I:
Proem.1, 164–65 and 200
Proem.2, 196
1.1, 74
1.7, 134
1.14, 170
1.29, 139–40
3.10, 183
4.4, 140–41
5.6, 176–77
7.2–3, 134–35
7.30, 172
9.35–36, 131–32
10.13, 182–83
10.48, 113–14
10.55, 114
10.56, 146
11.7, 200
11.11, 97
11.14, 84
12.18, 206n10

BOOK II:
Proem.4, 34
1.7, 76

3.30, 110
5.2, 29–30
6.13, 108
7.29, 171
8.1, 117–18
8.5–9, 162–63
9.22, 118–19n5
9.37, 114
9.41, 44–45
9.46, 50
9.50–51, 19–20
9.57, 197
11.22, 170
12.45, 54
12.50, 57
12.77, 6 and 183–84
12.81, 6

BOOK III:
Proem.2, 60
Proem.3, 102–3
Proem.5, 35
1.20, 180–81
1.34–38, 52–53
1.57, 136

1.67, 136
2.19, 36
2.28, 137
2.48, 137
4.7–8, 86–87
4.18, 113
4.32–34, 81–82
5.39–40, 78–79
7.27, 180
8.5, 49–50
8.51, 137–38
9.2, 148–49
9.11, 138
11.29–46, 53
11.47, 47
11.51, 53
12.1, 138–39

BOOK IV:

2.47, 80
4.47, 85–86
6.19, 113
6.20, 104–5
7.38, 79
10.6, 58
10.15, 3 and 58–59
10.21–22, 57–58
10.39–40, 48–49
11.11, 142
11.17, 11
11.25, 85
11.27, 56
11.45, 55 and 66–67n31

BOOK V:

3.24, 50–51
4.22, 167

5.2–3, 178–79
5.43, 75
7.6, 48
7.12–13, 147–48
8.1, 108
8.4, 126
8.29–30, 144
8.33, 145
8.43, 145–46
9.21, 141
9.28–29, 184–85
10.16, 83
11.19–21, 47
12.29–30, 149–51

BOOK VI:

Proem.1, 109
Proem.2, 189–90
Proem.3, 36
Proem.5, 36
1.6, 189
2.5–6, 77–78
2.39, 166–67
5.38, 146
7.41–43, 168–70
8.48, 151
9.7–8, 142–43
10.11, 10
10.12, 44 and 143
10.13, 116–17
10.17, 185–86
11.13, 171
12.25, 66n25

BOOK VII:

7.4, 109
7.8, 56–57

A Note on the Author

Judith Dundas received her doctorate in English from the University of Wisconsin and is a member of the English Department of the University of Illinois. Her published work has centered on the relationship between poetry and painting in the Renaissance.